The
Perfect Being

I0887117

Praise for *The Perfect Being*

"Mystics' works and teachings are critical to the understanding of Persian history and culture. Aziz O-Din Nasafi's writings offer insight into this often superficially understood facet of Persian arts and humanities. Dr. Amir Sabzevary has made the content of this valuable text accessible and enjoyable to read through his valuable translation and his in-depth contextual knowledge of the subject. While he prepares us to receive and experience the aesthetic complexities of Nasafi's writings, Dr. Sabzevary encourages the reader to transcend the 'intoxicating' beauty of the writings to become aware of their transformative and inspirational potentials."

—Shadieh Mirmobiny, PhD, educator of art history and humanities, Folsom Lake College

"When life in the modern world appears to have lost meaning, decency, humility, and purpose, we can turn to sources of ancient wisdom for reassurance and direction. *The Perfect Being* points to the spiritual heart as a source of power, intelligence, and understanding. Those who understand the mystical way of life will be touched. Those who seek to understand will be encouraged and renewed."

—Staci Tye, professor of humanities, Laney College

"The teachings in Nasafi's classic text are meant for both the ears of the head and the ears of the heart. Dr. Sabzevary's beautiful translation will educate those curious about the Sufi path. With profound gratitude, we receive this erudite and precious contribution to English-language scholarship on Iranian Sufi mysticism, which will enlighten generations to come."

—Emily Hanlon, lecturer of humanities, San Francisco State University

"For anyone walking a spiritual path, guideposts along the way are necessary. The words of Aziz O-Din Nasafi offer us that much-needed guidance, and Dr. Amir Sabzevary's translation allows simple and straightforward access to that wisdom. Perhaps one of the greatest gifts offered in this book is the notes Dr. Sabzevary provides throughout, giving deep insight into the meaning behind Nasafi's words. These notes greatly contribute to making this book a profound and meaningful read."

—Alyson Collom, instructor of humanities

"Sabzevary brings his considerable knowledge of literary Persian and classical Sufi hermeneutics to bear, making the text accessible for a contemporary audience while remaining true to Nasafi's original work. In a modern world often devoid of true religious spirit, Sabzevary's translation and commentary call us back into the luminous world of medieval Sufism—serving as a reminder that even hundreds of years later, the hidden wisdom continues to live on—if only we have the eyes to see. This illuminating translation not only gives us eyes to see but points beyond the senses altogether—to a realm of peace, compassion, and unity. Nasafi's words of wisdom in this text reach across time and space, ultimately inviting us, too, to live into the essential teachings of the Sufi path."

—Cassie Lipowitz, senior lecturer of religious studies, Notre Dame de Namur University

"In contrast to the Sufi literature currently available in the West, such as the poetic and intellectual renditions of Rumi and Ibn Arabi, Aziz O-Din Nasafi's *The Perfect Being* is a lucid and straightforward manual on Sufism. Professor Sabzevary's eloquent introductory notes explain the Islamic and Persian cultural etiquette that serves as the cradle that holds and protects these ideas, as without embodying these cultural nuances, Sufi ideas can only serve superficial functions. The resulting translation is one of the most accessible and comprehensive works on self-knowledge available in English."

—Brian Johnson, professor of religion and philosophy, Merced College

"*The Perfect Being* calls across time and place, beckoning those with ears to hear to turn away from the chaotic din of contemporary culture to contemplate the perennial path of wisdom instead. The distractions of everyday life are as old as time; mercifully, the healing wisdom found in *The Perfect Being* is older than time itself. It is our good fortune that both writer and translator/editor of this grace-filled volume possess the vital depth of understanding to bring this ancient wisdom to their respective time and place."

—Carolyn D. Collom, professor of humanities and religious studies, Laney College

The Perfect Being

Selections from the Classic Islamic Text

Aziz O-Din Nasafi

Translator and Editor
Amir Sabzevary, PhD

Fortress Press
Minneapolis

THE PERFECT BEING
Selections from the Classic Islamic Text

Copyright © 2021 Fortress Press, an imprint of 1517 Media. All rights reserved. Except for brief quotations in critical articles or reviews, no part of this book may be reproduced in any manner without prior written permission from the publisher. Email copyright@1517.media or write to Permissions, Fortress Press, PO Box 1209, Minneapolis, MN 55440-1209.

Scriptures taken from the Holy Bible, New International Version®, NIV®. Copyright © 1973, 1978, 1984, 2011 by Biblica, Inc.™ Used by permission of Zondervan. All rights reserved worldwide. www.zondervan.com The "NIV" and "New International Version" are trademarks registered in the United States Patent and Trademark Office by Biblica, Inc.™

Scripture quotations marked ESV are from the ESV® Bible (The Holy Bible, English Standard Version®), copyright © 2001 by Crossway, a publishing ministry of Good News Publishers. Used by permission. All rights reserved.

Cover image: Anna Poguliaeva / Shutterstock.com
Cover design: Brad Norr

Print ISBN: 978-1-5064-7281-2
eBook ISBN: 978-1-5064-7282-9

Contents

The Second Treatise

The Third Treatise

The Fourth Treatise

The Fifth Treatise

The Sixth Treatise: On the Manners of Solitude

The Seventh Treatise: On Love

The Eighth Treatise

The Twenty-Second Treatise: On Heaven and Hell

The greatest Sin: *Fear*
The greatest Enjoyment: *Work*
The greatest Calamity: *Hopelessness*
The greatest Courage: *Patience*
The greatest Teacher: *Experience*
The greatest Secret: *Death*
The greatest Honor: *Faith*
The greatest Profit: *A Noble Child*
The greatest Gift: *Forgiveness*
The greatest Investment: *Confidence*

—ALI, COUSIN OF
PROPHET MOHAMMAD

Introduction

O, dervish! Know for sure that we are travelers and certainly we pass the time hour by hour. If there is wealth, it will pass, and if there is affliction, it will pass. If you have wealth, do not put your trust in it because it is unclear what will happen in the next hour. If you have affliction, do not be excessively sad because it is not clear what will occur in the next hour. You should try not to cause harm to anyone, and as far as possible, you should try to bring comfort.

—**Aziz O-Din Nasafi,** ***Maghsad al-ghasee***[1]

The Beginning

Roughly six hundred years after Christ, a young man in the Arab world named Mohammad was consumed with the perplexing questions of identity, meaning, and purpose. He shared his heartfelt existential inquiries with the elders of his community, Jewish and Christian sages, and philosophers. But no answer that he received brought peace or comfort to his curious, restless mind and troubled heart.

As the world around him proved itself far too insufficient to adequately address the problems of a probing mind, a desperate heart, and a restless yearning spirit, he decided to seek solace and refuge in the darkness of a cave in Mount Hira, near Mecca. For almost twenty years, Mohammad journeyed to and from this cave consistently, as the exquisite solitude encompassed in darkness proved itself to be the only appropriate answer to his existential quandaries. It was there, in that solitude and quiet, that he expressed the most profound manifestations of despair, anguish, sorrow, joy, peace, understanding, and contentment.

It was not until the age of forty that a miracle transpired—God spoke to Mohammad through the angel Gabriel. This experience changed his life and completely transformed the Arab world, gifting it with a new religious tradition: Islam, which means *submission* or *surrender* to God's will. Although Islam was a new religion to Bedouin, Jewish, and Christian communities, Mohammad stressed that it was merely the continuation of the message given to people by Moses and Jesus. Mohammad continued to receive such miraculous revelations for the next twenty-two years, all of which were compiled in a book called the Quran, the sacred Islamic text.

As many listened to Mohammad's message during his prophetic career, some believed that it had a double meaning: one meaning could be heard through the *ears of the head* and the other through the *ears of the heart*. The former revolved around the "Letter of the Law," whereas the latter desired to experience the "Spirit of the Law."

That which can be heard through the ears of the head mostly deals with the literal understanding of Mohammad's message. It is concerned with religious faith and belief within the context of human conduct in the personal, social, and political worlds. It filters experiences through one's belief system, which is the product of one's history, religion, and social and political arenas.

That which can be heard through the ears of the heart symbolizes a space within the human being that can only hear things that are divine. It is about inspiration and the remembrance of the *God within*. Those who possessed such "ears" in Mohammad's time were called *Ahl saf'fa*, or "Brethren of Purity." They listened to Mohammad's message with the ears of the heart instead of the ears of the head. Like Mohammad in the early days of his life, they found themselves poor in spirit and plagued with the timeless existential questions of identity, meaning, and purpose. They felt and believed that their flesh imprisoned their spirits, that their minds were held hostage by the demands of the social and political worlds. Mohammad's message, they argued, was nourishing a part of them that had been neglected and yearned for a kind of experience that could not be disturbed or corrupted by space and time. They believed that they had found a man who was able to educate their hearts and spirits and set them free from the troubles of a world that often proved confusing, uncaring, cruel, and unjust.

The Sufis

"The poor in spirit" who became interested in the inner or esoteric approach to Mohammad's message came to be known as the Sufis. The word *Sufi* has been defined in a variety of different ways. Some have argued that it is derived from the word *suf*, which means "wool," as wearing a wool cloak was a symbol of simplicity and spiritual poverty. Others have argued that the word has its roots in the Greek *sophia*, which means "wisdom." Some have stated that Sufism has its origins in Islam, whereas others have claimed that it dates to Abraham, the father of the three monotheistic traditions, Judaism, Christianity, and Islam. Regardless of one's position regarding the definition and origination of Sufism, it is safe to say that it is the mystical dimension of Islam and that the Sufis are Muslim mystics.

These were the Saint Francis of Assisis and Theresa of Ávilas of the Islamic world who found themselves in a love affair with

God. They likened themselves to moths attracted to fire. They were willing to sacrifice everything, including life itself, to experience closeness and unity with fire. The Sufis would later call this desire and experience *fana fi-lah*, or "annihilation in God."

The Sufi teachers, or sheikhs, spoke in great detail about the difficulties of the path toward *self-knowledge* and becoming a genuine *seeker after truth*. They also warned that the path toward self-knowledge and God could not be traversed alone. Contrary to the Western approach of "doing it yourself," the Sufis, like most authentic esoteric traditions, cautioned that the spiritual journey is far too subtle and complicated and that the human being frequently is profoundly susceptible to self-deception; thus a guide is necessary.

The following tale is told by the great eleventh-century Persian Sufi Mohammad Ghazali, and it illustrates the manner through which the seeker falls prey to the subtle and cunning ways of self-deception and how such deception manifests itself inwardly and outwardly:

> A very devout and pious man was told that people had been engaged in worshiping a tree in a town not very far from his own. Knowing this to be an act of idolatry, he picked up his ax and set out toward the town to cut down the tree so that people may once again come to worship the one true God. On the way, however, he ran into the devil.
>
> "Where are you going?" asked the devil.
>
> "To the nearby town to cut down the tree so that people may worship the one true God," responded the man.
>
> "This cannot be done!" shouted the devil.

Angrily, the man slapped the devil to the ground and jumped on top of him. As he was about to behead the devil, the devil pleaded with the man to spare his life. In return, the devil promised to put two gold coins under his pillow every morning.

After some deliberation, the man agreed. As was promised, the man found two gold coins under his pillow the next morning, with which he bought groceries for his family and the poor in his town.

The man's joys and hopes soon disappeared when he discovered no coins under the pillow the following morning. Reasoning that the devil had probably forgotten and would most likely double the number of coins the next day, he went about his daily routine. No coins, however, were found the next day either. Frustrated and angry, he again picked up his ax and headed toward the town to cut down the tree. Again, he met the devil on the way, and as before, the devil asked, "Where are you going?"

"To cut the tree down," replied the man.

"You will not be allowed to do such a thing," uttered the devil.

The man slapped the devil again and again, but to his surprise, the devil remained unmoved. With a soft blow, the devil threw the man to the ground and was about to take his life. Helpless, the man asked, "Before you take my life, explain to me why I was victorious over you the first time and not this time."

"Because," said the devil, "last time, your intention for cutting the tree was for the sake of God, and this time it is for the sake of the gold coins."

This story illustrates that although the quest for self-knowledge and one's sense of religiosity appears to be profound and noble, it is plagued with selfish and corrupt intentions and motives. For this reason, the Sufis stressed the importance of a guide who can protect the seeker from subtle forms of false assumptions and self-deception.

The Sufis argued that there were two significant obstacles to the path to self-knowledge. The first was the immense cultural, social, and political forces that distracted the human being and kept them from asking existential and spiritual questions. The second obstacle was the profound tendency toward self-deception, forgetfulness, and sloth. To overcome these two hurdles, they demanded strict obedience to the guide, or sheikh. The seeker, or the *salik*, they argued, must be like clay in the hand of his sheikh. In the words of Nasafi, "Seekers must follow their sheikh's instructions without question, as they are like patients in the hands of a physician. If the patients do not observe the physician's remedy, they shall not be cured, and their illness may even worsen. Seekers cannot heal themselves through any other means except through the presence of the sheikh. The sheikh is the only physician able to rid the seekers of their ailments."

To this end, various physical, emotional, psychological, intellectual, and spiritual exercises were created for the seekers to follow, all of which were carefully overseen by the Sufi teacher. Sacred gathering places, known as the *khaneghah*, were also created, where the world and its troubles were never allowed to enter. Here the seekers would gather to pray and worship, listen to their guide's teachings and instructions, and perform various exercises as well as eat communally.

Aziz O-Din Nasafi

The eleventh through the thirteenth centuries were an exciting and vibrant period for Sufi thought and practice. The profound fragrance of Sufism rapidly spread throughout the Middle East and elsewhere. This period witnessed the speculative thoughts of such figures as the Ibn al-Arabi, better known as the grand sheikh of Sufism; Najm ul-Din Kobra; and Ghazali, as well as the highly symbolic, sorrow-and-love-filled poetry of Khayyam, Attar, Rumi, Sa'adi, Hafez, and Baba Taher.

There was, however, another important reason for the further blossoming and spread of Sufi thought and practice. For centuries, Iran (also known as Persia) had suffered one devastatingly sad political event after another. This impacted every aspect of Persian culture, society, philosophy, religion, literature, and psychology. Iran suffered horrible acts of cruelty and bloodshed at the hands of its own political regimes and witnessed the brutal and deadly invasions of the Arabs, Turks, Afghans, Greeks, and Romans. The incredible instability of physical, social, and political arenas gave birth to a negative outlook on life and the world. The Persians had become far too intimate with the wisdom of Jesus's words in Matthew 6:19–21: "Do not store up for yourselves treasures on earth, where moths and vermin destroy, and where thieves break in and steal. But store up for yourselves treasures in heaven, where moths and vermin do not destroy, and where thieves do not break in and steal. For where your treasure is, there your heart will be also." Or, as Nasafi put it, "Know for sure that there is no joy in this world."

This was the age and the culture that shaped the physical, emotional, intellectual, and spiritual lives of Aziz O-Din Nasafi and many others who desired to walk the Sufi path. Nasafi was a thirteenth-century Sufi teacher who was born in Nasaf, a city in Iran. Unfortunately, nothing about his youth and early adulthood is known. Later, in several of his writings, he briefly mentions, and only in passing, serving a Sufi teacher named Sa'ad al-Din Mohammad Hamouyee, who, before his death, permitted him to pass on the Sufi knowledge to others.

It is, of course, not surprising that so little is known about Nasafi's life given that Persian culture has always frowned on, with a great distaste, any expression, whether written or verbal, containing notions of individual uniqueness and self-importance. Some of the greatest Sufi teachers—such as Abu Saeed Abul-Khayr, Khaje Ansari, Hafez, Rumi, and Sa'adi, whose personal lives remain in a shroud of mystery—even refrained from the usage of the word *I*. As the saying goes, it is the message that is important, not the messenger. Close observation will reveal a significant amount of humility in the manner in which Nasafi refers to himself and his writings: "The community of dervishes asked of this beggar of God, Aziz O-Din Mohammad Nasafi, to put together a writing that would provide the necessary wisdom and guidance to seekers and a writing that would serve as their companion."

Of Nasafi's many works, two stand out as classical Islamic Sufi texts: *Kashf al hagha-egh* (Unveiling of truths) and *Inson al-kamel* (*The Perfect Being*). The former focuses on the seekers' journey toward self-knowledge, the nature of existence and God; fragmentation and unity; life, death, and resurrection; the nature of heaven and earth; the symbolism behind pilgrimage to Mecca. The latter text, which is the focus of this work, was composed at the request of both novice and advance students. It is a collection of treatises that discuss the nature of existence, the nature and the evolution of the soul, the relationship between the teacher and the disciple, and the practical aspects of the path, such as praying and fasting.

It is important to note that Nasafi's writings are not entangled in academic logic-chopping, mere memorization, or regurgitation. That exercise is best left to the modern-day academics, who amuse themselves with such tasks.

The Persian Sufi mystic poet Rumi, in his masterpiece *Masnavi*, asks, "Why didn't the donkey Jesus rode when he entered Jerusalem become an object of worship?" After all, the great prophet Jesus was seated on it! Rumi tells us the answer is quite simple: "Transformation is not possible by mere contact." In other words, wisdom cannot be attained through mere association with the wise. Most often, one simply gathers information and mistakes the possession of information for the possession of wisdom. Rumi describes these people as donkeys carrying books. Therefore, the art lies not in collecting these ancient pieces of wisdom but in knowing the proper *time* and *place* to execute them.

The consensus among Sufi practitioners is that parroting various aspects of the tradition without proper understanding will inevitably corrupt the teaching's real purpose and intention. As Nasafi eloquently states,

> O, dervish! Do not be concerned with acquiring knowledge and wisdom so that you may be called wise or looked upon as such. And do not perform too many prayers or acts of worship so that you may be called righteous or sheik. Know that these desires will cause great calamities and sufferings. Acquire only the necessary knowledge and perform only those acts of devotion beneficial to you on the Path. Concern yourself only with protecting your inner state from corruption. Also let your concern be in bestowing peace

upon others and not harming them. This indeed is where man's salvation lies.

Although his writing seems simple, a closer and more in-depth reading of it reveals the immense complexities of his thoughts and Sufism in general. Nasafi writes with the desire to intoxicate his readers with mysteries and complexities of what it means to be a human being. His writings and instructions are not meant to be merely read and enjoyed. Instead, they are meant to transform the reader's interior life and set the reader's heart ablaze! That is the mission of every wisdom tradition and every authentic teacher of wisdom: to purge their audience of everything that could become an obstacle to reflection, self-knowledge, and wisdom.

This Work and the Present Age

This leads to another point, which is that Sufi ideas were never meant for public consumption. Like all authentic esoteric traditions, it always dimmed itself to avoid visibility because it recognized the difficulties and the dangers one encounters on the path toward wisdom. Sufism unveiled itself and its mysteries only to those who were ready to be burdened by its physical, emotional, intellectual, and spiritual demands and hardships.

The emotions of dissatisfaction and despair are significantly amplified in the present age, when nearly all ancient wisdom teachings have been gutted out or dismissed as outdated and irrelevant. Despite all the exterior glimmer and glamor, the modern world has given birth to a contemporary human who is forced to stand alone in the desert of loneliness, isolation, meaninglessness, hopelessness, confusion, and despair.

Despite the terrible and devastating position that the contemporary world has placed the human individual in, it has given birth to exotic philosophies of life designed to create enlightened and hopeful mirages of meaning, identity, and purpose. This, of course, has been made possible through the immensely deceptive powers of advertisement and human gullibility, which mistakes the illusory nature of mirage for something real and of substance.

When something like Sufism or any other authentic esoteric school is popularized and turned into an organization, especially in secular-consumer-capitalistic culture, the intentions and actions of its leaders and followers become questionable. The reason quite simply is that it slowly begins to move from the original goal of *self-knowledge* and *selfless* service to its followers and ultimately humanity—if, of course, such a goal ever existed—into the field of *customer satisfaction*. As a result, the spiritual, intellectual, ethical, and moral principles within that tradition begin to deteriorate, and as time goes on, they are eventually moved aside and replaced by what is the essential component in any industrious and growing organization: *profit*. Profit in the current social environment can take any shape or form, such as emotional, psychological, intellectual, social, and financial. However, this shift takes place in such a subtle way—usually under the cloak of spirituality, religiosity, and righteousness—that it is rarely noticed. Therefore, those joining such organizations without clearly understanding what has given rise to their need to join or those who wish to be entertained and have little or no background in the field of *self-study* and *self-realization* become easily trapped in today's philosophical, religious, and spiritual markets.

As Nasafi puts it, "Over the years, people of the Path and people of the world have joined in sacred performances. Sufi sheikhs have always been again such public activities. Such activities are meant to entertain children. Dervishes must beware not to engage in such childish games."

The selections in this work are intended to familiarize modern readers with some of the core ideas, practices, and etiquettes of Sufism in its traditional form instead of the popularized one designed to fit the modern Western secular-consumer-capitalistic psyche. Due to the subject's enormity, this work can only provide a small footnote to the grand and complicated world of Sufi thought and practice. Regardless of how this work is read and perceived, it is hoped that it offers the reader glimpses into the world of Sufism that will inspire curiosity—and perhaps, on occasion, stings of reflection.

In the Name of God, the Merciful and the Compassionate

Introductory Treatise

Chapter One

The Law, the Way, and the Truth

(1)

The community of dervishes[1] asked of this beggar[2] of God, Aziz O-Din Mohammad Nasafi, to put together a writing that would provide the necessary wisdom and guidance to seekers[3] and a writing that would serve as their companion, as well as a symbol by which I could be remembered. It would be far too lengthy to write all that is necessary for seekers to know, but I have nevertheless undertaken the task asked of me. May God assist me in what has been requested of me to avoid any errors.

These sections have been written to help increase the trust and faith of beginners on the Path and those who are more advanced. Some of the sections, however, are such that only the advanced will find them useful.

(2)

Know that the Law is the Prophet's utterances, the Path is his deeds, and the Truth is what he witnessed or experienced.[4] The seeker must first thoroughly learn and understand the Prophet's sayings before setting foot on the designated Path so that he can be granted illuminations and unveilings, according, of course, to the degree of the seeker's effort and readiness.

(3)

O, dervish! Whoever accepts the Prophet's sayings becomes a member of the Community of Law Keepers. Whoever follows the Prophet in deeds walks the Path that he has designated. Whoever witnesses and experiences what the Prophet witnessed and experienced becomes a member of the Community of Truth.

(4)

O, dervish! The Perfect Ones are those who have accepted the Prophet's sayings, follow him in deed, and witnessed and experienced what the Prophet had seen and experienced. They are given the title "the Perfect Ones." They are the ones who can guide the masses. Any person or group who lacks any of the mentioned qualities is imperfect. They are indeed the unworthy ones and in need of guidance.

(5)

O, dervish! Know that most people only have a human being's appearance. In truth, they are not human beings, but only asses and cows, foxes and tigers, and snakes and reptiles. Trust that this is so. Only a few are truly human beings in every town, and the rest only appear to be so.

Chapter Two

On the Perfect Being

(6)

Know that the Perfect Being is a person who possesses the Law, the Way, and the Truth. Stated differently, the Perfect Being has four qualities: right speech, right ethics, right action, and gnosis.

(7)

O, dervish! The task of all those on the Path is to attain and realize those four qualities. Those who have actualized those four qualities have obtained self-knowledge. Know that many have entered and traveled the Path but have failed to reach the Destination: the Truth.

(8)

Know that the Perfect Beings have many different names and attributes. They are known as the Sheikh,[1] the Guide, the Wise, the Reflector, and the Transformer. They are also known as the Prophet. They can be Jesus, who raises the dead, or Khizr,[2] who drank from the waters of eternal life, or Solomon, who knew and spoke the language of the birds. Know that the world is never empty of a Perfect Being and that there is never more than one. Many possess gnosis, but it is only the Perfect Being who is the essence of all gnosis. When the Perfect Being departs from this world, another with the same qualities replaces him. The world, therefore, is never without a Perfect Being.

(9)

O, dervish! The entire world is like a box that holds all of creation. However, no created thing knows itself or the container in which it exists except for the Perfect Being, from whom nothing is hidden and veiled. Only the Perfect Being knows and perceives the essence of everything and keeps watch over all.

(10)

O, dervish! When Perfect Beings enter the presence of God and realize Him, they come to understand the nature and the essence of every creature and its purpose. Most importantly, they come to realize that there is no task greater than bestowing tranquility and peace upon people. They converse with people and invite them to the gates of wisdom and its ways, and bless them with tranquility and peace. In this way, people shall live in peace and be safe from the calamities of this world. Hence whoever follows this Path inherits the Prophet's wisdom.

(11)

O, dervish! Perfect Beings realize that the noblest of all tasks is to heal the world by leading the people towards righteousness, cleanse them of their evil ways and habits through kindness and compassion, and call them towards affirming God's unity. They speak to people about the instability and corruptibility of the world, worldliness, and greed and demonstrate the nobility of the dervish-hood and its doctrine of poverty.[3] And finally, Perfect Beings invite people toward compassion and mercy rather than anger, hatred, and revenge. In this way, not only shall they live in peace and harmony, but they shall also establish a community in which nothing but kindness and mercy govern.

(12)

O, dervish! Creating such communities has been the desire of the Prophet, saints, and sages. It is they who provide and guide people towards the path of peace and tranquility.

(13)

O, dervish! God's mercy rains upon everyone and everything. The Prophet's mercy is bestowed upon humanity, and sages' mercy is bestowed upon the true and genuine seekers. This was what the Prophet and sages invited people to hear. Now that the greatness of Perfect Beings has been revealed, know that their powers are limited. And despite all their attributes, they cannot change everything that they want. Therefore, their powers are limited and imperfect. Being as it is, they cannot but live in this world and its ways as best as they can. Their perfection, however, lies in their wisdom and conduct.

(14)

O, dervish! The Prophet and the saints have wanted many things to be a certain way, but it never happened. They also wanted many things not to be the way they were, but those things remained contrary to their desires. Thus it is evident that the Perfect Beings and the imperfect ones, the wise and the ignorant, the king and the slave, are all weak and incapable and must accustom themselves to the ways of the world. Some of the Perfect Beings realized that regardless of their efforts, the world and its ways remain unchanged; there is no other task better than renunciation. Hence they detached themselves from everything and chose to live in freedom.

Chapter Three

On Perfect Freedom

(15)

Know that Perfect Beings have perfected four attributes: speech, ethics, conduct, and divine knowledge. But the liberated Perfect Beings are those who have perfected eight attributes: speech, ethics, conduct, divine knowledge, detachment, solitude, contentment, and being anonymous. Whoever perfects each of these eight attributes attains perfection and freedom, completeness, and maturity.

(16)

O, dervish! Those who possess the first four qualities, and not the last four, are perfect but do not have perfect freedom. Those who have the last four qualities, but not the first four, have complete freedom but are not perfect. Now that you know the qualities of those who have both perfection and freedom, you must also know that there are two schools of the perfected ones.

The first school observes solitude,[1] contentment,[2] and seclusion so that their identities remain unknown. The second school observes surrender, reflection, and contentment to be satisfied with whatever God places in their lot. The aim of both schools, however, is attaining detachment and freedom. Some have argued that detachment is achieved through solitude, contentment, and seclusion, whereas others have argued that detachment is attained through surrender, reflection, and satisfaction with whatever God places in one's lot.

The school that observes solitude, contentment, and seclusion argues that the world and its occupants are the creators of distraction and fragmentation. For this reason, they cut themselves off from the world and its occupants. Hence they neither accept nor become occupied with worldly things. If they find themselves amongst worldly people by chance, they run away from them as if they are in the presence of hungry lions, wolves, tigers, and snakes.

The school that observes surrender, reflection, and contentment argues that human beings do not know what genuinely benefits them. There are times when harm lies in the very things that they enjoy most, yet they are not aware of this. And there are times when their benefit lies in the presence of things that they do not want. Having realized this, this school chooses to remove their own will, thus choosing surrender. As a result, they became neither joyous nor sorrowful with the gain or loss of wealth or status. They graciously receive everyone who enters their presence—worldly or otherwise.

This beggar of God has observed both schools' principles and has found that they provide various paths that can be beneficial and harmful.

Chapter Four

On Speech

(17)

Know that speech[1] has a profound impact on the listener. Seekers who have not been in the presence of a sheikh's utterances will never reach the Destination or attain anything of value. All forms of asceticism, spiritual exercises, and codes of conduct have been created so that the seeker can become worthy of being in the company of a wise person. Once seekers become worthy of this, they will be able to reach their Destination.

(18)

O, dervish! Seekers shall benefit more from the presence of a wise teacher, even if for only a moment, than engaging in a hundred or even a thousand years of praying and ascetic exercises. No one can reach the Destination without being in the company of a sheikh, even if the seekers possess great talents and have immersed themselves in spiritual exercises.

(19)

O, dervish! Many have come in the presence of a sheikh but have gained nothing. They either have no desire for this Path and do not seek it or are inwardly sleeping and cannot hear. The wise cannot communicate with those who do not desire this Path. A community is established only when two or more persons want the same thing. In this way, communication and community are born.

(20)

Now that you know the definition of communication, you must speak little and refrain from answering questions that are not asked of you when you enter the presence of dervishes. If you are asked a question to which you do not know the answer, you must quickly say, "I don't know," without any feeling of shame. If, on the other hand, you do know the answer, you must make your response short and to the point. You must never become engaged in arguments, as that shows your pride and arrogance. You must never desire to sit above anyone and must always allow others to sit above you. Finally, you must never make demands of anyone.

(21)

O, dervish! Always keep your manners and be polite.[2] Impoliteness, regardless of where you are, is always wrong. The task is to live in solitude without making any demands on others, for making demands is against dervishes' etiquette. You must never worship idols and must not make anything your idol.

(22)

O, dervish! If you wish to remain in the community of dervishes, you must embrace and accept their ways. Remember that any task that becomes a habit becomes an idol, and you want to refrain from becoming an idol worshipper.

(23)

O, dervish! Do not engage in unnecessary tasks and those that do not bring solace or benefit to the community of dervishes. Let no task become a habit, for then it becomes an idol. The task of breaking a habit and destroying an idol is only possible for those on the Path.

Chapter Five

On the Journey

(24)

Know that the task of those on this Path is to journey to and in God.[1] There is an end to the journey to God but not to the journey in God. In the journey to God, the seeker passes into nonexistence[2] and enters God-consciousness. He is born in God. There he acquires new sight, hearing, speech, and wisdom.

(25)

O, dervish! When seekers realize that all existence is an aspect of God, the journey to God ends, and the journey in God begins. The journey in God consists of being born in Him. At this stage, the true nature of all things is revealed to the seekers and nothing, in either this world or the other, will be veiled from them.

Some have suggested that the journey in God has no end because human life is limited, making it impossible for the seeker to know everything. This may indeed be true given the infinite nature of God's knowledge and wisdom.

(26)

O, dervish! Now that you know what the journey consists of, also know that the Sufis and the Community of the Wise have said that God reveals Himself and His attributes according to the inner development of each person. On the other hand, the Community of Unity[3] argues that there can be no journey to God since He occupies all spaces.

The First Treatise

Chapter Twelve

On the Evolution of the Human Spirit

(1)

Know that the community of dervishes asked of this beggar of God, Aziz O-Din Mohammad Nasafi, to put together a work regarding the human being's exterior and interior formations. That is, to discuss the evolution of the soul and its purpose. May God assist me in what has been requested of me to avoid any errors.

(22)

Know that the Community of Law Keepers has argued that those who accept the teachings of the wise and follow them enter the stage of faith and are given the title "Believer." When they receive and observe the laws of the wise with their entire being and spend their nights in prayer, they enter the stage of devotion and are given the title "Worshipper." By continuous worship, they free themselves of worldly and bodily desires. They then ascend to the stage of austerity and are given the title "Ascetic." Observing the ascetic tradition and principles, the essence of both this and the other world is unveiled before them, and they become self-realized and enter the stage of gnosis and are given the title "Gnostic." Those who ascend to this reach this stage become the guardians of their people and are given the title "Prophet." This is the path of spiritual evolution.

(23)

The Community of Law Keepers has said that there are nine stages to the soul's evolution, which are dependent on the degree of virtue and gnosis of the soul. No soul, regardless of its effort, can evolve beyond the capacity that was given to it at the time of its birth. A soul shall attain its full potential so long as its life is not wasted while in the physical body.

(24)

The Community of the Wise,[1] on the other hand, argues that everyone attains illumination according to his or her effort. Wisdom is given according to the degree of effort one puts on the Path. The more effort one puts on the Path, the higher and more advanced stage one will reach. Hence it is impossible to tell the capacity and the stage of any soul.

(25)

The Community of Unity argues that the evolution of the human soul is unlimited. If human beings were to live a thousand years during which time their only task was to gather wisdom, they would find something new every day, for the knowledge of God is unlimited. The highest attainable stage is when the soul leaves the physical body so that it can once again assume its proper place. All things are journeying to reach the stage of a human being. Once achieved, that journey is complete. The human being must then journey towards perfection. The journey is complete only when perfection is attained. However, one can never achieve perfection, for perfection lies in having complete knowledge of God, which is impossible. Attaining perfection, therefore, is relative. However, the Community of Law Keepers and the Community of the Wise argue that human perfection lies in the right speech, right ethics, right conduct, and gnosis. In acquiring these, one will also gain wisdom of the world, wisdom of the afterlife, wisdom of the self, and wisdom of God.

Chapter Thirteen

On the Number of Souls

(26)

The Community of Law Keepers and the Community of the Wise argue that people have either three, four, or five souls. Those who have three souls are the imperfect ones, those who have four souls are the mediocre ones, and those who possess five souls are the perfect ones.

(27)

O, dervish, know that I believe that all people, perfect or otherwise, possess only one soul. But each soul resides in a different stage, and each stage has its unique name. People's error lies in this: they mistake the various stages and their names for the number of souls.

(28)

O, dervish, both the body and the soul are always evolving, ascending, and going through various stages until they attain perfection, if, of course, they remain free from corruption. Everything in this world is always in a state of fluctuation; things are sometimes descending, sometimes ascending, contracting,[1] or expanding.[2] The road to the Path is built upon hell, and everyone from prophets to kings, from masters to slaves, must go through it. Some shall walk upon this road joyously and effortlessly because they observe the teachings of the wise and therefore do not busy themselves with the world and its occupants. They are detached and are thus free from greed, lust, and envy. There are those, however, who fall on this road and crawl to the Path. They are in constant sorrow, strife, and struggle, for they do not pay heed to the advice of the wise. This is so because they become busy with the world and become consumed by the fires of greed, lust, and envy.

Chapter Fifteen

On Advice

(33)

O, dervish! You must not allow your heart[1] to become attached to the world as it is always in a state of flux. No sooner does the world appear one way before it disappears and changes into something different. The world resembles the waves of the sea that always come and go, and the wise never try to find security amidst the waves.

(34)

Choose the Path of dervishes,[2] for they are the wisest people. They have chosen this Path, as they know that behind every worldly joy lie a hundred sorrows. The wise never choose one joy that is accompanied by a hundred sorrows.

(35)

O, dervish! Realize that we are all travelers, and we too must depart when our time has arrived. Know that whatever the moment brings, whether it is joy or sorrow, it will pass. Hence do not feel secure if you possess wealth and do not become sad and frustrated if sorrow has entered your lot, for you do not know what the next hour will bring. The wisest thing to do is to be the bringer of peace and solace to others.

The Second Treatise

Chapter One

On the Essence of Being

(1)

Know that the community of dervishes asked of this beggar of God, Aziz O-Din Mohammad Nasafi, to put together a work regarding the subtleties of unification, unity, and union. May God assist me in what has been requested of me to avoid any errors.

(2)

Know that being necessitates existence, and that is the providence of God alone, without whom nothing would exist.

(3)

People differ in their knowledge[1] of God. Some are imitators. They simply believe and follow blindly. Then there are those who rely on intellect and reasoning. Finally, there are those who patiently wait until God finds them worthy of divine revelation.[2]

Chapter Two

On the Community of Imitators

The Common Person

(4)

This community utters the existence and the unity of God with their tongues. They "know" that the world has one Creator who is omniscient, omnipotent, and pure. They know that God knows the hearts of all people and the intention behind all their actions. Those in this category have attained their faith not through contemplation nor divine revelation but rather through hearing it from others. That is why they are called the imitators.[1]

(5)

O, dervish! This community's faith is not the result of experiencing the divine presence and His utter dominion over all things or understanding all things while in a state of worship. They cannot know anything other than what they acquire through their senses.

(6)

Know that this is the lot that most people occupy and consequently experience pain and sorrow, greed, and envy.[2]

Chapter Three

On the Uniqueness of the Community of Intellectuals

(7)

This community utters God's existence and His unity not only with their tongues but also with their hearts. They have attained the certainty that the world has one Creator who is omniscient, omnipotent, and free of all impurities—that He is the beginning and the end, who knows the hearts of people and their intentions. The Community of Intellectuals[1] has attained its faith through the light of reasoning and understands that the entire creation depends on God for its sustenance.

(8)

O, dervish! Those who have attained realization understand that their souls cause all of their movements. The fingers that move the pen are moved by the hand, which is moved by the arm. But they are all governed by the soul. Think of everything as such! Everything has a cause, and that cause is God, from whom all comes to life. That is why it has been said that if you know yourself, you will know God.

(9)

O, dervish! Know that it is from God that cause and effect arise. Therefore, God allows some of His creations to reside at higher stages of being than others. They are all part of God, though God is none of them.

(10)

O, dervish! Know that all created things in the heavens and the earth stand as equals before God, and this is because there is no place where He is not.

(11)

O, dervish! Even though some created things stand at higher levels than others, they are all nevertheless equal before God.

(12)

Now that you know that all things are created and sustained by and through God, also know that God has many different treasures to bestow. They are such things as existence and life, health and security, wealth and intelligence, knowledge, and wisdom. He gives and takes away these treasures to and from anyone He wishes. No one has access to such treasures except God.

(13)

O, dervish! Know that God gives His treasures to whomever He pleases.[2] When these treasures are given, trust replaces greed, contentment and surrender replace effort. All desires end as God's will reigns. Finally, prayer and supplication will replace all worldly desires and affairs.

Chapter Four

On the Community of Revelation

(14)

This community utters the existence and the unity of God not only with their tongues but with their hearts as well. They have attained the certainty that God is the sole creator of this world. This community has achieved its faith through what God has revealed to them.

(15)

O, dervish! This community has passed through all the stages and has thus reached the presence of God. They have realized God through the certainties of both the mind and the heart. They are therefore called the Community of Unity, for they see and know nothing but God.

(16)

The Path begins with separation or detachment from the world and gradually moves towards unification or seeing God in everything. It then moves towards unity, where one realizes the interconnectedness of all things since they rest in God. But longer indeed is the journey from unity to union, where seekers see themselves within all things. This should be the aim of all seekers.

(17)

O, dervish! There are two kinds of veils. One which covers God from us, thus making it impossible to see and know Him. And that which covers everything else so that nothing but God is seen and known.

(18)

Know that the meaning of unification is to bring many things into one. This is done in two ways: unification through knowledge[1] and unification through action.[2]

(19)

Know that Unity's meaning is to bring together two or more things, and this is called Oneness. There is no separation or fragmentation in Unity. This should be the aim of the seeker.

(20)

O, dervish! When multiplicity has vanished, there is no longer a seeker or separation or even a union. All that remains at this stage is God.

(21)

O, dervish! God's presence is constant. Seekers, however, assume and imagine otherwise. However, upon transcending their assumptions and imaginations, they will realize God's presence and everlasting existence.

(22)

The Community of Unity argues on behalf of God's sole existence and the impossibility of anything else but God to exist. Even though there is only one Being, God, He has numerous physical manifestations, and these are in the form of sight, speech, hearing, and feeling. Since the very essence of this Being is light, then all its manifestations are light. This is called "light upon light."

(23)

Know that the essence of this Being is Light. Since the entire existence is its manifestation, every aspect of creation is, therefore, an extension of this divine light.

(24)

O, dervish! This divine light must be reached and experienced so that idols, fragmentation, and confusion can be removed. My sheikh, Hamouyee, once said, "When I reached this limitless ocean of divine light, which has no beginning and no end, it placed me in such a state of awe that I could no longer sleep, work, or eat. I could not even speak of my experience with anyone."

(25)

O, dervish! Those who do not reach the sea of light and have not drowned in it will never understand the true meaning of Unity. Those who do not reach the stage of Unity will not attain the presence of God and thus will not experience the essence of creation. Many claimed to have seen and experienced this sea of Light in their illusion, but blind, they entered this world, and blind, they departed.

(26)

O, dervish! Those seekers who have reached this sea of light and are drowned in it are at peace with everyone and everything and constantly bestow compassion and mercy[3] upon all. They aid all in need and see everyone as being on the path to

God. A friend told me this tale: "For many years, I preached and invited people towards God, but no one accepted this invitation. Disappointedly I turned towards God for comfort and saw that all people were standing in His presence. They were all speaking to and hearing from Him."

(27)

O, dervish! Proper education[4] is not in making the wretched happy, or giving talent to the untalented, or revealing truths to people. Instead, it is in removing their improper and destructive habits. This will help them live healthier lives and make them more compassionate and just towards one another. Everyone is a mixture of good and bad attributes, and all that they need is guidance, not truth.

(28)

O, dervish! Nothing in this world is bad, but things are perfect when they are in their proper place. However, the judgments of "bad" and "good" arise only when something is not in its rightful place.

Chapter Five

Another Community within the Community of Unity

(29)

There are two schools of thought within the Community of Unity. One argues that there is only one being, God, and nothing but God exists.[1] The other argues that God has an actual existence, but the world exists only through imagination.[2] God exists but cannot be seen, and the world, which is seen, does not exist. According to the second school of thought, the world is a mirage that lingers between existence and nonexistence.

The Third Treatise

Chapter One

On Three Groups of Human Beings, Who Are a Mixture of Material and Spiritual

(1)

Know that the community of dervishes asked of this beggar of God, Aziz O-Din Mohammad Nasafi, to put together a writing regarding the soul's creation, its stages its evolution, and its ascent and descent. Also, to discuss if the soul attains perfection and reaches its proper stage of being or whether its potential and possibilities are predestined and will not increase despite one's will and effort. May God assist me in what has been requested of me to avoid any errors.

(2)

Know that the human soul, which once existed in the heavenly world, has been sent to this lower world so that it can evolve into perfection and once again return to its divine origin. Since perfection could not have been attained without housing the soul in a proper container, the physical body was given. Human beings, therefore, are composed of both body and soul. The body belongs to a lower world, whereas the soul belongs to a higher or celestial world. Through God's command, the body and soul came into existence.

(3)

Know that a group of people in this lower world have not yet realized that they are travelers, and their journey is towards perfection. Since they have not attained this realization, they have become occupied with the pursuit of base or lower desires. That is the desire for security, food, and family. These desires have deceived them, thus making them idol worshippers. However, another group of people have realized that they are only travelers and have come to journey from this lower world to the higher world and attain perfection. But since they have not entirely given themselves to the task, they too have been deceived by their desire for outward beauty, wealth, and status, making them idol worshippers of a different kind. These are the six branches of worldly desires, and there are no other branches besides these.

(4)

O, dervish! As the latter three branches (outward beauty, wealth, and status) gain more power, the former three branches (security, food, and family) become less important. But know that aside from these six idols, there is one more: the ego.[1] All six branches exist only to please the ego, which is the greatest of all idols. Although the other six idols can be removed, it is nearly impossible to break the ego.

(5)

Some know that they are but travelers in this lower world and are here to attain perfection. They are, in fact, working towards that end. And of those who have reached perfection, some labor in perfecting others. In contrast, many are merely working towards perfecting themselves. Human beings usually belong to one of these three groups: those consumed by their ego, those working towards perfecting themselves, and those who labor in perfecting others. Of these three groups, some are human beings, while others have only the appearance of human beings.

(6)

O, dervish! There is only one way to attain perfection: through proper education, observation, and application. Whoever follows this guideline shall reach the goal.

(7)

O, dervish! Those who are not adequately educated regarding the Path but enter the circle of dervishes may, in fact, journey to God, but they will never become the right instrument for God to journey in them.[2]

Chapter Five

On the Placement of Spirits

(15)

O, dervish! Those who did not accept the Prophet and his teachings are human beings but only in appearance.[1] They are, in fact, lower than the four-legged animals. These creatures are not worthy to enter the celestial realm, the angelic house of the pure and the faithful. Without wisdom and faith, it is impossible to enter the higher world. The spirits of those who lack faith shall remain within this lower realm.

(16)

O, dervish! God created all the souls with utmost purity and sent them to this lower world to attain perfection. But some lost their way, as worldly pleasures deceived them.[2]

(17)

O, dervish! The souls descended so that they could ascend to perfection. Therefore, there is a purpose in both their descent and their ascent. But each soul has a definite stage of perfection beyond which it cannot go.

Chapter Six

On the Soul's Fate

(18)

O, dervish! Know that each soul can only evolve to its predestined stage.

(19)

O, dervish! No one can enter celestial stages through one's own efforts; otherwise, one could become a mystic, then a guide, and finally, a prophet. This is simply not so. One cannot enter a stage for which one was not created unless it is willed and destined by God.

(20)

O, dervish! Each soul is given a specific capacity and potential beyond which it cannot evolve.[1] Each soul is given a body and a specific time line to occupy that body. That body is given the definite number of breaths it will take, the amount of food that it will intake, the nature of its thoughts, its language, and its learning. Know that God has designed each soul to be as such.

Chapter Seven

On God's Destiny

(21)

Know that there was only God. He existed in eternity, and through His will, the angelic and the heavenly realms came to be. The angelic realm is the realm of celestial bodies, and the heavenly kingdom is the realm of spiritual bodies. Everything then is the essence and manifestation of God.[1]

(22)

Some have argued that God, through His eternal wisdom, willed all things to have a definite potential, capacity, and purpose.

(23)

O, dervish! Know that some people want to attain God's wisdom, while others wish for the wisdom of His justice. However, if what they desire was not written on the tablet of their destiny, they will attain neither His wisdom nor the wisdom of His justice.

Chapter Eight

On Traversing the Path

(25)

Know that the ascent or descent of the spirit is a subtle thing. The bridge that must be crossed is stretched across hell. It is finer than a hair and sharper than a razor. At times, one is on the bridge; other times, one is above the bridge; and still other times, one is under the bridge. Some pass this bridge with ease, some fall and crawl their way across it with much pain and suffering, and some never cross the bridge and fall into hell. The ascent and descent of the human spirit are the same way. Spirits must come into this lower world and must pass through it. Hence some pass through this world effortlessly, some fall and crawl their way through it, and some never pass through it.

Chapter Nine

On Human Beings, in Whom Are Contained Both This and the Other World

(26)

Know that all that exists in this and the other world exists in each human being. Human beings, therefore, are books that reveal the nature of this world and the other.

(27)

O, dervish! When the human spirit descends, it is as if the sun has set, and when it ascends, it is as if the sun has risen. Therefore, to descend represents night, and ascension represents day. When the spirit descends, everything is blanketed by darkness, and nothing can be seen. But when the spirit soars towards the heavens, everything is uncovered and reveals itself. Human spirit, therefore, has two qualities: ascension and descension.[1]

(28)

O, dervish! There is a community of people whose spirits have descended into darkness due to weakness and ignorance. As a result, they have no experience and knowledge of the light. There is also a community of people whose spirits have ascended due to will, strength, knowledge, wisdom, and grace. It is this community that has reached the light.

(29)

O, dervish! Becoming educated on this Path demands that seekers work hard and make every effort to humbly sit at the feet of a sheikh. In this way, they shall attain purity of mind and body. Only in this way will their spirits become worthy of light. When the body and the spirit become pure, they can properly receive and apply knowledge and wisdom. This gives birth to gnosis, or divine knowledge. It is like a fire that burns all false and impure thoughts and imaginations.

The Fourth Treatise

Chapter One

On the Creation and Resurrection according to the Community of Wisdom

(1)

Know that the community of dervishes asked of this beggar of God, Aziz O-Din Mohammad Nasafi, to put together a work regarding the ways of the Community of Wisdom. May God assist me in what has been requested of me to avoid any errors.

(3)

The Community of Wisdom has said, "God first created Intelligence. Everything else sprung from that."

(5)

O, dervish! Human beings, who were the last entity to be created by God, came from the fruit of the Tree of Creation. When they attained Intelligence, it became apparent that the seed of the Tree of Creation was Intelligence. For that which came last also came first. Hence Intelligence existed in both the beginning and the end.

(6)

O, dervish! Intelligence was the first thing created by God, and creation came to be because of it. For this reason, it has been said, "God created human beings in His own image."[1]

(7)

O, dervish! The many forms of Intelligence and beings in the higher world are free from corruption and are thus purer because they are closer to the original Intelligence.

(8)

Know that first is God, then Intelligence, then existence, and lastly, nature.

(9)

O, dervish! First is God. The prophets and the sages are His manifestations. Then there is Intelligence, whose fruits are the wise and the learned. Then there is ego, whose fruits are the kings and wealthy. Then there is nature, whose fruit is humanity. In the first stage exists God, in the second stage exists Intelligence, in the third stage exists the ego, and in the fourth stage exists nature. These are the stages of this and the next world.

(10)

O, dervish! The Communities of Law Keepers and Wisdom have both said the breath that arises in and from the lower world is different from the breath that arises in and from the higher world, as the latter is rooted in God's will.

Chapter Two

On the Intelligence and Structure of the Lower World

(12)

O, dervish! The differences in people have to do with how they were created and what they have been destined to achieve in this lower world.[1]

(13)

O, dervish! Now that you know that the fate of each human being was written before coming into this lower world, learn to be content and satisfied with what God has put in your lot and surrender to His will. The poor must live with poverty, and the wealthy must live with wealth. But they both must also live with the pain and suffering that poverty and wealth bring them.

(14)

O, dervish! Know for sure that there is no joy in this world.

Chapter Three

On Resurrection

(15)

After it has left the body, the soul shall enter the higher realm if it has attained perfection. If, however, it has not, it shall remain in the underworld, which is hell.[1]

(16)

Beings in the celestial realm are continually acquiring more wisdom and are in a constant state of worship. Therefore, the seekers' task is always to seek more wisdom so that they, too, can be in a state of continuous worship. In this way, when it is time for the soul to leave the body, celestial beings shall pull the soul towards themselves. The soul is attracted to whatever it has desired and acquired. When the spirit reaches the higher realm, it enters the world of eternity. There it will taste peace and joy. The more purity and wisdom it has acquired, the higher the stage to which it enters. The Community of Law Keepers is incorrect in stating that each soul has a definite stage and that the circle completes itself once that stage has been reached. This community argues that the soul resides in a definite stage of existence before acquiring a body. Upon descending into the lower world, the soul continuously attempts to regain its former status, which it cannot transcend. However, the Community of Wisdom argues that the more wisdom the soul acquires, the higher it shall evolve on the ladder of existence.

(17)

O, dervish! Those who purify and perfect their spirits reach the stage of perfection. At this stage, when the soul leaves the body, it shall enter the presence of God and bask in His glory unto eternity. This is the paradise that has been promised to the perfected ones. Whoever attains this stage attains absolute peace and joy. Hell is the residence of the imperfect ones. If their imperfection is due to a lack of knowledge and wisdom, they shall never attain freedom from their suffering. However, if it is due to the lack of purity, they shall become free with proper training.

(18)

O, dervish! The soul may be in six states after its release from the body, divided into simple or complex states: simple and pure, simple and impure, complex and pure, complex and impure, complex and perfect, or complex and imperfect. These are the different states of the soul after its liberation from the body.

Chapter Four

On the State of the Soul after Its Release from the Body

(19)

Know that the soul which has not acquired wisdom and purification before being liberated from the body will remain within this lower realm and will not enter the celestial kingdom. Some masters have argued that souls that stay in this lower realm shall enter different bodies. In this way, they shall pay and suffer accordingly for the wrongs that they had committed while in the body. Some will acquire the bodies of animals, some plants or other forms, until each has attained the proper knowledge.[1] Once the appropriate knowledge is acquired, it will become worthy of entering the celestial realm.

(20)

Other masters, however, have argued that souls cannot enter different bodies. They simply remain in this lower realm without being housed in physical forms.

(21)

Still others have suggested that the souls that have remained in this lower world are indeed the evil spirits that appear from time to time to whomever they want and whenever they want.

(22)

Some masters have argued that evil spirits do not exist. Such notions are the work of imagination. Evil spirits are those people who have never entered the presence of a sheikh. Such people are animals—no, they are lower than animals in whom intelligence has not yet been born.

Chapter Five

On Advice

(25)

O, dervish! This beggar has traveled to many places and has been in the presence of many masters. He has served them and observed their teaching with much care. He has greatly benefited from the teachings of these great teachers. This beggar's inner vision was born through their presence, thus enabling him to witness the celestial realm that expanded his spiritual vision. For this reason, this beggar only took friends who possessed wisdom.

(26)

O, dervish! Those who only know one branch of learning have a limited vision and are unable to appreciate the teachings of the prophets and sages. Those who possess knowledge and wisdom have a great vision. Those who have studied these writings with care have given birth to their inner vision and have found all necessary for this Path.

(27)

O, dervish! Do not be concerned with acquiring knowledge and wisdom so that you may be called wise or looked upon as such. And do not perform too many prayers or acts of worship so that you may be called righteous or sheikh. Know that these desires will cause great calamities and sufferings. Acquire only

the necessary knowledge and perform only those acts of devotion beneficial to you on the Path. Concern yourself only with protecting your inner state from corruption. Also let your concern be in bestowing peace upon others and not harming them. This indeed is where man's salvation lies.

(28)

O, dervish! Anyone who did not purify his lower self[1] became a slave to wealth and status. Know that these desires destroy the faith of the seeker. Desires of wealth and status resemble a human-eating dragon that drowns and devours thousands of people. To not have such desires is to be free. Of course, there is no such thing as absolute freedom, but one may be relatively free.

(29)

Whether they are prophets, sages, kings, or ordinary people, everyone in this world is a prisoner to attachments. Some are prisoners to one attachment, some to two, some to ten, some to a hundred, and some to a thousand. No one in this world is free from attachments. The less one is attached to things, the freer one is. And the more attachments one has, the more pain and sorrow he experiences. Such is the way towards suffering.

(30)

O, dervish! If you cannot be free, at least try to be content and accept what God has placed in your lot.

The Fifth Treatise

Chapter One

On Traversing the Path

(1)

Know that the community of dervishes asked of this beggar of God, Aziz O-Din Mohammad Nasafi, to put together a writing regarding the Path, its nature, the stages therein, and the intentions of the seeker on the Path. May God assist me in what has been requested of me to avoid any errors.

(2)

Know that traveling the Sufi path is not an outward activity but an inward one. It not only means a journey to God but also God's journey in you.[1]

(4)

O, dervish! Know that there are many inner levels on this Path that reveal themselves as the seekers enter each new stage of understanding. The seekers pass from the lower world to the higher world once they witness their qualities and attributes. Upon entering the higher world, they become deputies of God in the lower realm. Their words become the words of God, and their deeds become the deeds of God. At this point, righteousness and wisdom are born.

(5)

O, dervish! Wisdom is obtained in this lower realm. Seekers must realize that the journey on this Path consists of their continuous quest to find all that is hidden within themselves. They cannot become deputies of God and they cannot help humanity unless they have come to know themselves completely.[2] How can those who cannot govern themselves rise to govern others? Error and falsity arise when people assume to possess something that they do not possess, which then leads them to experience pain and sorrow. When a seeker has finished traversing through all the inner levels, then the journey has come to an end.

(6)

O, dervish! It has become clear that you are the Seeker, you are the Path, and you are the Destiny. When all your attributes and qualities are realized, then the never-ending journey of God in you begins.

Chapter Two

On the Intention of the Seeker on the Path

(7)

O, dervish! The seeker must never say, "I seek God," or "I seek to purify myself and my conduct," or "I seek knowledge or gnosis," or "I seek divine secrets and illumination," for each of these is a spiritual stage that the seeker must become worthy to enter.

(8)

O, dervish! There are stages of being as there are stages that the tree must go through to reach maturity. The gardener's task is to plow the ground, rid it of weeds, and water the tree to help it reach maturity. The seekers must do something similar. They should discipline themselves and strive toward becoming human beings rather than just looking like they are. Like a tree, seekers must go through the stages of spiritual growth and maturity to become worthy of divine secrets.[1] Once deemed worthy, they shall witness things beyond their imaginations. Those who are not on the Path and have never experienced the subtleties of the Path will never comprehend this. While seekers have breath in their lungs, they must make great effort, work hard, be strong-willed on this Path, as there is no end in the wisdom of God.

(9)

O, dervish! All the stages that the tree must travel to reach maturity already exist in the seed. However, it needs an experienced and caring gardener to ensure that the tree reaches those stages. Similarly, purity, compassion, wisdom, illumination, and divine secrets exist in the human being. But they will become actualized when one has entered the presence of a wise and experienced teacher.

(10)

O, dervish! All wisdom is within you. Whatever you seek, seek it within, never without.[2] The knowledge that passes from your ears into your heart is like taking water from other people's wells and pouring it into your own well. And because the water in your well is still, it becomes contaminated and infected with diseases.

(11)

O, dervish! The water in such a well is the birthplace of sickness. That sickness manifests itself in pride, arrogance, and the inescapable desire for wealth and status. You must become the well that quenches the thirst of others. The more you give, the more will be given to you.

(12)

O, dervish! Those who seek the truth must stay on this Path until the Water of Life springs forth from their hearts.

(13)

O, dervish! The journey on the Path is only possible with the presence of the wise, without whom nothing beneficial can be attained. The fruit that grows in a desert without an experienced gardener is much different from a fruit that ripens under an experienced gardener's care. Similarly, seekers who have been trained under a wise teacher's care are much different from those who have not.

Chapter Three

On the Attainment of Wisdom through the Purification of the Body

(14)

Know that the gospels of the prophets and the saints are designed to teach people right thinking, right speech, and right conduct.[1] Once they have fully and adequately observed the teachings, all their expressions will be without error. People's interiors manifest themselves through their external behavior. Corrupt outward action, therefore, is an indication of a corrupt inner state. In other words, people's interiors are the containers, and their outward deeds are the contents. That which is poured into the container takes the shape of the container. If the container is ill-shaped, then the contents too represent themselves as such.

(15)

O, dervish! Know that the external forces impact one's inner world. And the inner world affects the outer world. Through strict self-discipline of the lower self and being in the presence of a sheikh, seekers are made proper both inwardly and outwardly. The soul resides between two worlds: the world of being and the world of nonbeing. The body is of the world of being, whereas the soul is of nonbeing, the angelic realm. The invisible world, the world of nonbeing, is always pure and free of impurities. It is a world in which the soul is never troubled, for it resides in divine light. The world of being is the world of lust, desire, and greed. It is a dark and decadent world that darkens the soul. If the body or the world is purified, then the soul becomes purified. In this way, whatever exists in the invisible world, which is the angelic world, begins to manifest and reveal itself in the heart of the seekers. Seekers, therefore, become a two-way mirror in which both worlds see and experience themselves.

(16)

O, dervish! Know that the invisible world and the seekers' souls have many different levels, and each level is different from the others. Seekers, whose hearts are cleansed and hence pure, regardless of their religious faith, shall experience illumination through dreams, divine intoxication, revelation, and divine knowledge. Illumination occurs in dreams more often than wakefulness because the five senses cause distraction. In sleep, the senses, which provide an entrance for lust and desires, are no longer operative and lose their powerful force. Thus the spirit can attain illumination during those hours. Seekers must choose solitude, seclusion, and strict self-discipline for their bodies to experience divine revelations in dreams.

(17)

O, dervish! Every seeker is different. Some will attain illumination with little work, while others will achieve nothing even after years of spiritual training.

Chapter Four

On the Three Groups of People

(18)

Know that God in His mercy created every man differently and gave each a special and unique talent. The order of the universe is such that every man was created to fulfill a specific task.[1]

(19)

O, dervish! Some are weak-willed and consumed with base desires, and some are strong-willed and consumed with noble desires. Some want the pleasures of this world, and some desire the satisfaction of the next. Still, some choose nothing but God. These are the three groups of people. Those who want God are strong-willed with noble desires and are the most dignified of people. They are the seekers who fulfill their purpose. The rest are weeds and thorns.

(20)

O, dervish! There are four essential kinds of knowledge that seekers of the Path must possess. Knowing one's destination, desiring self-knowledge, understanding the nature of the Path towards the Destination, and recognizing a real guide. Without these four insights, the journey will be impossible to make. Know that the aim and the goal of seekers are to perfect themselves. Some have said that it is not the seeker but God who is on the journey; others have said that it is the seeker's spirit on the journey. Some state that it is the seeker's Intelligence that is on the journey. Still others say that it is the light of God that is on the journey. According to this beggar of God, it is the seeker's soul and the divine light within that is on the journey. Different names such as the ego, the spirit, the heart, intelligence, and divine light have been called this light.

Chapter Five

On the Path to the Destination

(21)

It has become apparent to this beggar of God that there is continuous learning on this Path. It requires strict self-discipline, reflection, and contemplation. Seekers must enter the *khaneghah* to be trained by their sheikh to learn the laws of the Path and its subtleties. There they shall learn the knowledge of the Path and the teachings as instructed by their sheikh. They must abandon all their learnings and completely submit to their sheikh. Some, of course, argue that there are two paths towards the destination. The first path consists of the seeker acquiring what is essential and then applying it to understand it fully. This path is for seekers of the Law. The second path demands strict self-discipline, prayer, and meditation. This path is for seekers of the Way.[1]

(22)

O, dervish! Seekers are those who not only learn something new each day but also forget what they have learned.

(23)

O, dervish! Some seekers have said, "We are going to learn the art of painting to design the entire universe on our hearts. In this way, our hearts shall become the tablet of secrets." Other seekers have said, "We are going to learn the art of polishing our hearts so that our hearts can be purified with self-discipline and meditation. In this way, our hearts shall become transparent and reflect all the designs and wisdom that are contained both in the worlds of being and nonbeing. Know for certain that what our hearts shall reveal is much more flawless than what is written in all the books." However, it will not be possible to possess all forms of knowledge, as human life is limited. But with discipline and constant effort, it is possible to polish and purify one's heart so that it can reflect the wisdom of both this world and the next.

(24)

O, dervish! There is only one Path towards the goal. However, if there were two paths, know that the Path of discipline, constant work on oneself, and meditation is the safest and the easiest.

Chapter Six

On the Level of the Common Person

(25)

Know that children must accompany their parents to worship until they have reached maturity. This agreement between children and their parents is called Islam, which means "to surrender." When children have reached an age where they can reflect, they must without a doubt take to heart and do six essential things: (1) to faithfully believe that there is only one God and Mohammad is His messenger and that all his teachings are God's teachings, (2) to comply with the religious laws and the instructions therein, (3) to be aware to not stray from the straight path, (4) to repent and vow never to make the same error, (5) to learn a trade through which one's livelihood does not contaminate and corrupt one's faith, and (6) to be virtuous so that one's livelihood is from an uncontaminated source.

(26)

O, dervish! These six essential components are the basic guidelines for common and ordinary Muslims. Those who wish to reach the level of an ordinary believer must observe these six laws. But those who desire to become part of the Community of the Elect must go beyond and follow the teachings of the Elect. Teachings of the Elect are designed for the seekers and are attained through rigorous discipline, study, meditation, and application.[1]

Chapter Seven

On the Conditions of the Journey

(27)

Know that six conditions must be present for the seeker on the journey: (1) renunciation from seeking wealth and status, (2) bringing humanity peace by abstaining from injuring anyone with words or conduct and seeing them as an extension of oneself, (3) seeking solitude and seclusion, (4) annihilating one's ego, (5) fasting,[1] and (6) attaining supernatural powers.

Chapter Eight

The Pillars of the Path

(28)

The first pillar is that seekers must always follow their sheikh's instructions. The second pillar is that they must respectfully and lovingly serve their sheikh. In this way, seekers reach the destination with the least amount of hardship. Know that as the seekers increase their service, respect, and love towards their sheikh, obstacles are overcome with greater ease. However, if there is a speck of decrease in service, respect, and love towards the sheikh, seekers shall not reach the destination and shall be abandoned midway.

The third pillar is that seekers must be obedient to their sheikh. Seekers must follow their sheikh's instructions without question, as they are like patients in the hands of a physician. If the patients do not observe the physician's remedy, they shall not be cured, and their illness may even worsen. Seekers cannot heal themselves through any other means except through the presence of the sheikh. The sheikh is the only physician able to rid the seekers of their ailments.

The fourth pillar is that the seekers must renounce their own judgments and thinking and only rely on the instructions of their sheikh so that they can reach their destination. The fifth pillar is that the seekers must never argue or protest the commands or the sheikh's wishes, for they are not yet able to discern between the useful and the useless, the beneficial and the harmful, the good and the evil. Indeed, the story of Moses and Khizr[1] illustrates this point.

(29)

O, dervish! There are many utterances and forms of conduct that seekers may assume to be proper, but their sheikh may think otherwise. It may be the case that certain statements and conduct may seem improper to the seekers, but their sheikh may think otherwise. Since it is only the sheikh who knows what is truly beneficial and harmful, seekers should renounce their own judgments and simply follow the sheikh's advice in all matters.

(30)

O, dervish! Protesting and argumentation will only bring about discord between the seeker and the sheikh and darkens their relationship.

(31)

The sixth pillar is the firm and constant observance of the previously mentioned pillars. Nothing good can be achieved in this world or the next without honoring them.

(32)

O, dervish! It is only with hard work and dedication that anything of value can be achieved.

Chapter Nine

On Veils and Status

(33)

O, dervish! If seekers observe the pillars[1] and the conditions of the Path, the veils that hide the truth shall be removed and they shall attain the highest level of awareness. Four veils hide the truth from the seekers: (1) desire for wealth, (2) desire for status, (3) desire to follow and imitate the ways of the uninitiated, and (4) desire to act in ways that are contrary to the etiquette of the Path. Seekers must also follow the following four principles: (1) right speech, (2) right conduct, (3) right morals, and (4) right learning. They must also be mindful and aware of (1) the world and its ways, (2) the afterlife and its ways, (3) the presence of death, (4) the devil and its ways, (5) the angels and their teachings, (6) the Prophet and his teachings, (7) the ability to understand their sheikh's instructions, (8) the various layers of the ego, and (9) God and His commandments.

(34)

O, dervish! To discern if a command is from the devil or angels, the ego or God, and fully comprehend the teachings of the prophets and sages is indeed a profoundly difficult task.

(36)

Know that the seekers' main task is to renunciate, suffer, and sacrifice everything that the Path prohibits. In this way, the veils are removed, and perfection is attained.[2]

(37)

O, dervish, whoever removed the veils is in a constant state of worship and prayer.

Chapter Ten

On Training

(38)

A sheikh initiates seekers by shutting their eyes, tying their legs, keeping them hungry and thirsty during the day, and depriving them of sleep during the night. In this way, the seekers' egos are annihilated, and they can gradually find rest and peace in and through the sheikh. The sheikh, then, teaches the seekers divine wisdom so that they can enter God's presence.[1] Therefore, the sheikh's intention behind sewing the disciples' eyes shut, tying their legs, keeping them hungry and thirsty is so that they could enter God's domain. Sewing the seekers' eyes is to place them in darkness, closing their mouths is to make them recluse, and forcing hunger and thirst on them is to remove the obstacles that keep them from witnessing the celestial realm. This is the stage of salvation and freedom.

The Sixth Treatise

On the Manners of Solitude

Chapter One

On Obedience and Disobedience

(1)

Know that the community of dervishes asked of this beggar of God, Aziz O-Din Mohammad Nasafi, to put together a writing regarding the forty-day training.[1] We shall discuss what during this training must be eaten and how much and which chants should be performed and in what manner. May God assist me in what has been requested of me to avoid any errors.

(2)

Know that there are three fundamental aspects to the community of Sufis. First is attraction, where the seekers are pulled toward God by God. The second is that the seekers must traverse the Path through their own effort and self-discipline. And third is ascent, which seekers attain through the mercy of God. Only those who have obtained these three aspects are deserving of the title sheikh.

(3)

O, dervish! From the beginning to the end, there are a total of ten different stages. Each stage has its own unique components of attraction, path, development, and instruction. The knowledge and recognition of right and wrong, obedience and disobedience, is indeed an arduous task. That is why the seekers must never rely on their own thinking and judgments but rather accept their sheikh's advice without hesitation or doubt. The seekers must be trained to realize that every stage demands its own specific training, which is only known to the sheikh. Specific training in one stage may be an obstacle in another stage. Hence right and wrong, obedience and disobedience have different meanings in different stages. For instance, before attaining faith or wisdom, sleeping, eating, and desires are all wrong and blasphemous on the Path, but such acts are indeed virtuous after the seekers attain faith and wisdom. That is, the seekers must reach a stage where God becomes their eyes and ears, their tongue, and hands. At this stage, God inspires all the seekers' actions.

Chapter Two

On the Conditions of the Forty Days' Training

(4)

The first condition is that the sheikh must permit the seekers to observe the forty-day training in a secluded space. Every seven to ten days, the sheikh shall visit the seekers to inspire, comfort, and encourage them and answer any questions that they may have.

(5)

The second condition is time and place. That is, these forty days must take place at a time when it is not too hot or too cold. The room in which these forty days take place must be completely dark and away from people and noise. Also, only the sheikh and cook shall be allowed in the room during these forty days.

(6)

The third condition is that the seekers must always keep their ablution and renew it whenever the prayer time arrives.

(7)

The fourth condition is fasting, which must be observed for forty days.

(8)
The fifth condition is to eat minimally. It is only the sheikh who can determine what the portion of each meal shall be.

(9)
The sixth condition is speaking as little as possible. The seekers are only to speak to the sheikh or the cook.

(10)
The seventh condition is that the seekers must sleep no more than eight hours at night.

(11)
The eighth condition is being mindful of one's thoughts. The contents of one's thoughts fall into four categories: divine thoughts, angelic thoughts, egoistic thoughts, and satanic thoughts. All these different categories have their own unique and specific signs by which they can be recognized.

(12)
The ninth condition is the negation of all categories of thought. During these forty days, the seekers must not become occupied with any forms of thoughts, whether divine or satanic. All thoughts that enter their consciousnesses must be negated and annihilated. At all times, the seekers must only follow the instructions of their sheikh. If seekers have had any thoughts or dreams, whether in sleep or waking, they must immediately be shared with the sheikh in private.

(13)

The tenth condition is being in a constant state of *zikr*. After performing the prayers, seekers must become engaged in nothing but the continuous repetition of the *zikr*—"La ilaha illa-llah" (There is no god but God).[1] The seeker must chant this aloud and always be present and acknowledge that they are engaged in affirmation and negation.

Chapter Three

On the Manners of Remembrance of God (*Zikr*)

(14)

Know that *zikr* for the seekers is as milk is for the infant. They must receive the *zikr* from their sheikh. Before performing the *zikr*, the seekers must first renew their ablution and perform the prayer of thanksgiving and then sit in the direction of the House of God.[1] Some have suggested that it is better to sit cross-legged as one performs the *zikr*. Others have said that one must sit on one's knees, resembling the praying posture. Our sheikh and his disciples all sat cross-legged.

The *zikr* must be performed aloud while the eyes are closed. Despite the seekers' best intentions, the *zikr* is initially performed by simply uttering it. The seekers, however, must continue with the *zikr* until it thoroughly penetrates and engages their hearts. They must be mindful that with every "la ilaha illa-llah," their hearts feel a subtle ache. After a few days of performing the *zikr* loudly, the seekers will notice that their hearts no longer experience pain, signifying that the words have penetrated the heart and that the heart is engaged in the *zikr*. The dervishes who are proficient in the art of *zikr* can easily notice whether it has penetrated their hearts, where divine mysteries are revealed. There are many benefits to this exercise that, unfortunately, cannot be put into words.

Chapter Four

On the Ascent of the Sufis

(15)

Know that the body is a veil, and upon death, the soul is freed. The ascent of prophets is in two manners: they either ascend with their bodies or without. However, their descendants, the saints, and sages have only one form of ascent, and that is without their bodies.

(16)

Our intention was not to discuss the ascent of the Prophet but the ascent of the community of the Sufis. Also to intensify the seekers' desire for God and to train them to be mindful of their own deaths and afterlives.

(17)

O, dervish, to observe, reflect, and know what becomes of oneself after one has left this physical life is indeed a difficult task. The ordinary person is uninterested in this. If they did care about their condition in this and the next life, they would spend day and night trying to attain insight into their condition, especially their condition once they leave their body.

(18)

Know that the ascent of the Sufis consists in the seekers' souls leaving their bodies while awake. Once their souls have been freed, the seekers shall see what awaits them in the afterlife. They witness this while still alive. They shall also see the condition of those who are in paradise as well as hell. At this stage, what the seekers knew intellectually, they now know through the eye of certainty.[1] They shall see some souls exist in the first heaven, some in the second heaven, and the seat of the prophets, which is the throne of heaven. Each soul can only attain what it was destined to achieve. They shall further see souls leaving the bodies that housed them and entering their destined realm.

Once a soul witnesses everything in its destined realm, it shall enter the body that housed it, remembering everything they have experienced. Some retain their experiences and share them with others, whereas others forget. Those who are not properly trained cannot remember their experiences, as it would be far too intense for their body and mind. There are, however, those who, due to proper training, are fully conscious of what they are experiencing. These passages can only be understood by those who have tasted such experiences. The souls of some stay in the heavens and circle it for two days, some others for three days or longer. The maximum number of days that a soul can remain in the various realms of heaven is twenty to forty days.

(19)

Our sheikh, Hamouyee, once said, "My soul roamed the heavens for thirteen days and then returned to the body. In those thirteen days, my body was simply a corpse, and those who were present also said that my body was motionless for those days." Another Sufi master had said that his soul was in the heavens for twenty days while his body just lay there. Another sheikh said that his soul was in paradise for forty days, and when he came back, he remembered everything that he had experienced.

(20)

It has been said that each person's soul can only reach the level for which it was destined. The Sufis argue that it is only the Prophet who reaches the throne of the heavens.

The Seventh Treatise

On Love

Chapter One

Introduction to Love

(1)
Know that the community of dervishes asked of this beggar of God, Aziz O-Din Mohammad Nasafi, to put together a writing regarding the nature of love and its stages. And to also discuss what compassion is. May God assist me in what has been requested of me to avoid any errors.

(2)
Know that those engaged in the remembrance of God fall into four categories: the imitator, the devotional, the compassionate, and the lover. We shall explain each of these categories so that the seekers can better understand.

(3)
The imitators are engaged in *zikr* in a very superficial way. Their tongues utter the words, but their hearts are consumed with worldly desires. There is, nevertheless, some benefit in this, however little that may be.

(4)
The devotionals utter the words with the knowledge that their hearts are not present or engaged. Knowing this, they, through intense religious emotions, try to awaken their hearts.

(5)

The compassionate are entirely consumed with the *zikr* and cannot bring themselves to engage in anything else. When there is a worldly obligation, they must force themselves to turn their hearts towards the temporal activity. This state of nearness to God is rarely achieved. Only lovers understand the true meaning of this. The lovers always speak of their beloved and cannot endure separation. They always talk about the beauty of their beloved and abstain from all things except their beloved.

(6)

The lover's heart is completely consumed and taken over by the contents of the *zikr*. To the lover, the phrase "There is no god but God" becomes a reality.

(7)

O, dervish! There will be times when the beloved so consumes the lovers that they forget not only the beloved's name but also everything else that is not the beloved.

(8)

The stages are then as follows: first is desire, second is devotion, third is compassion, and fourth is love.[1]

(9)

O, dervish! To wish to converse with someone, there must first be the desire. With the intensification of desire comes devotion. With the intensification of devotion comes compassion, and with the intensification of compassion comes love.

(10)

O, dervish! If the Beloved comes to you, honor Him. To keep Him is to make sure that you hold in your heart nothing but Him. Empty your heart of everything except Him.

Quatrain:

Love entered and became like blood to my veins and skin
It emptied me of me and filled me with God
God consumed every particle of my being
Only a name remains of me; the rest is He.

(11)

O, dervish! Love is a light for seekers and a saddle for travelers. Whatever the intellect has acquired, love burns in a moment. Love purifies the lover through and through. Seekers can observe the forty-day training a hundred times, but it is the lover who shall travel farther.

(12)

O, dervish! Of true love, we cannot write in a way that the people will comprehend. If they read of true love, they shall call it blasphemy. I shall therefore write of a sort of love that resembles true love.

Chapter Two

On the Levels of the Shadows of Love

(13)

Know that there are three stages to false love, better known as the shadows of love. The first is that the lovers continuously think of the beloved and circle the beloved's house as if it is the house of God. They continually keep watch of the house just in case their beloved appears. At the mere appearance of the beloved, their restless and broken hearts find peace. Indeed, it is only the presence of the beloved that can cure their hearts.

(14)

Even when the beloved appears, the lovers find that they cannot endure her presence. Their bodies begin to shiver, and they lose the ability to speak. There are also times where the fear of seeing the beloved causes the lovers to lose consciousness.

(15)

O, dervish! Love is a fire that strikes the heart and burns it. This fire enters from the eyes and travels to the heart to make it a home for itself.

> *If it were not for the heart, where would love reside?*
> *And if there was no love, for what use is the heart?*

The flames of this fire spread through all the particles of the body, burn what is impure, and make the heart so sensitive, soft, and delicate that it cannot endure the sight of the beloved. The fear is that the image of the beloved will annihilate the lover. That is why when Moses asked God if he could see Him, God responded, "You cannot endure My presence."

(16)

O, dervish! Lovers prefer separation to union at this stage, for there is much comfort in this. They have images of their beloved within them and speak and hear from the beloved all day. At times, the beloved caresses them and takes them into the state of expansion[1] and at times hides from them, taking them to the state of contraction.[2] Others see the expansion and contraction of the lovers without knowing or understanding what has caused them.

(17)

When the beloved has entirely occupied the lovers' hearts and has removed everything but itself, then all the hearts' gates shut to prevent anything foreign and impure from entering. It reaches the point that in eating, drinking, sleeping, or coming and going, the lovers imagine that it is not them but the beloved who is engaged in all these activities. When the lovers are freed from the sorrow of separation and acquire the strength to be in the presence of the beloved, they attain courage and become liberated from fear.

(18)

Know that some have said that the fire of the beloved burns the lovers' hearts until they have become delicate and spiritual. The presence of the beloved consumes the lovers' hearts and makes them its home.

(19)

O, dervish! As this beggar sees it, when the heart is entirely consumed by the beloved, all that the lovers see is the beloved. They cannot even see themselves, for they have ceased to exist. The search, separation, union, fear, hope, contraction, and expansion all vanish at this stage.

(20)

O, dervish! Those who do not love have not been cleansed and purified by love. Those who have been consumed by love cannot even describe any aspect of the beloved. Such hearts cannot help but blossom goodness.

The Eighth Treatise

Chapter One

On the Ethical Codes of the Sufis

(1)

Know that the community of dervishes asked of this beggar of God, Aziz O-Din Mohammad Nasafi, to put together a work regarding Sufi ethics. May God assist me in what has been requested of me to avoid any errors.

(2)

Know that the first code is that the seekers must always keep their ablution,[1] and each time they renew their ablution, they must perform two prayers[2] of thanksgiving.

(3)

The second ethical code is that the seekers should always carry their prayer rugs with them so that as they reach each destination, they can perform two thanksgiving prayers.

(4)

The third ethical code is to divide the day and night into prayers, as every moment requires a prayer. For example, there is a prayer of eating, a prayer of sleeping, and a prayer of walking. In this way, the seekers can protect their time and their lives from being wasted in forgetfulness.

(5)

The fourth ethical code is to perform twelve prayers before midnight and three before dawn.

(6)

The fifth ethical code is to perform various incantations after having finished the prayers just before dawn.

(7)

The sixth ethical code is to perform two morning prayers and follow them with various incantations. The seekers must then engage in spiritual exercises without leaving their prayers. They must be mindful not to utter even a single word concerning worldly affairs. For the Sufis, this is a profoundly valuable period in which unveilings take place.

(8)

The seventh ethical code is traveling. The seekers should never remain in any city for too long and must continuously be on a journey so they can experience its hardship as well as serving and honoring those whom they meet. They may come upon sheikhs from whom they can receive many blessings.

Chapter Two

On the Benefit of Traveling

(10)

The seekers must never travel alone.[1] They must travel with no more than four people and no less than two. They must choose amongst themselves a leader and respect and honor whatever decisions and choices that person makes. When they come upon a *khaneghah*, the dervishes' gathering place, they must ask for the person in charge of the *khaneghah* to be granted permission to enter. Once permitted, the *khaneghah* becomes their resting place. There, they must make their ablution and perform two thanksgiving prayers. They must then meet the dervishes and honor, respect, and serve them. If they are asked questions, they must make their answers short and brief. They must never respond to questions they have not been asked. They must stay in the *khaneghah* for three days and then ask whether they can leave for their original destination.

(11)

O, dervish! Those who enter the *khaneghah* shall not leave it without permission. Whatever they want, they must ask the person who runs the *khaneghah*.

Chapter Three

On the Codes of Conduct in the *Khaneghah*

(12)

Seekers must enter the *khaneghah*[1] with their right foot first and leave the *khaneghah* with their left foot.

(13)

O, dervish! In the *khaneghah*, they should talk and walk quietly and softly so that those in contemplation or sleep are not disturbed.

(14)

O, dervish! Everyone in the *khaneghah* has a specific task, and they must do that task with utmost sincerity and attention. They must never involve themselves in other people's business unless they have been given permission to do so.

(15)

O, dervish! Those who reside in the *khaneghah* must be aware of one another's inner state so that if one of the residents is undergoing a particular hardship, others can offer their assistance. It is a community where everyone must help one another. They must hide the faults of others and only reveal their good qualities. The younger seekers should always seek answers from the elders, and the elders should always give their advice in private. The elders should never respond to a question beyond the inquirer's capacity to understand, for that can cause more harm than benefit.

Chapter Four

On Causing Another Dervish Sorrow

(16)

If a dervish's words or actions have caused hurt and sorrow[1] to another dervish, he must, in a heartfelt and gentle manner, share it within the community of dervishes and in the presence of the sheikh. Such admissions should never occur without the sheikh's presence, for then the hurt would simply increase. If the accused can provide a reasonable answer for his action, the accuser must accept and forgive the other. If the accused cannot provide a sufficient response, he must then ask for forgiveness. They must sit together and place their hands on each other's shoulders. This must occur in the presence of all the dervishes. If there is a singer present, he must chant a devotional song, as there is much benefit. This act of sharing within the community of dervishes is instructive to everyone present.

Chapter Five

On Ecstatic Dancing

(17)

If ascetic exercises and disciplines, such as dancing,[1] cause a dervish to become ill, either physically or mentally, the community of dervishes must quickly find a remedy. One of the best treatments is to have someone with a pleasant voice sing a devotional chanting accompanied by a unique drum called *daf*. This action, however, must take place only in the presence of dervishes and not in public or before those unfamiliar with the Path.

(18)

O, dervish! Over the years, people of the Path and people of the world have joined in sacred performances. Sufi sheikhs have always been against such public activities. Such activities are meant to entertain children. Dervishes must beware not to engage in such childish games.

(19)

O, dervish! The sacred dance must always be performed at the right time and the right place.

(20)

O, dervish! If a sheikh decides to stand while ecstatic dancing is taking place, then the rest of the dervishes must stand. When the sheikh invites someone to the center, only that person must occupy that space. If the sheikh decides that everyone must participate in the center, then everyone should honor his instructions. If the sheikh sits or places his cap on the ground, the rest must do so, except those suffering from physical ailment. If a dervish during the ceremony suddenly enters a mystical state, the sheikh will rise, and the rest of the dervishes must do so as well unless he orders them otherwise. Those present must always respect and agree with the sheikh's instructions, which is a sign of true brotherhood.

Chapter Six

On Eating

(21)

Dervishes must sit appropriately at the dinner table. They must honor their elders by not sitting above them. They must begin eating only after the elders have begun and must not eat with greed. They should only look at their plates and not gaze at other people's plates. They must take small bites and entirely swallow that bite before taking another. If they eat from a communal dish, they must only eat the part facing them. If a part of their food falls on the table, they should not put it into their mouth but instead pick it up with their left hand and place it at the corner of the table. They must not finish their food until everyone is finished eating. Before eating, they must first wash their hands and, after eating, their hands and mouth.

(22)

O, dervish! You must read something about the lives of the great Sufi teachers daily.[1] In this way, you will acquaint yourself with the degree to which they exercised patience with others, their spiritual exercises and disciplines, and how they prayed. Everyone must have a place of seclusion where they can contemplate what they have learned.

Chapter Seven

On Asceticism and Discipline

(23)

Dervishes must observe strict self-discipline and ascetic exercises until the age of forty. After that, they must reduce the level of their spiritual practices until the age of sixty. After sixty, they must converse with the people of the heart. The greatest of disciplines is to serve a sheikh.[1]

Chapter Eight

On Speech

(24)

O, dervish! Speech has profound benefits.[1] Whatever the seekers attain, it is because they have entered the presence of a sheikh. All forms of asceticism and exercises have been created so that the seeker can become worthy of entering a sheikh's company. Once the seekers become worthy of this, they attain everything. When they become worthy of entering a sheikh's presence, all evil traits are removed and replaced by noble characteristics. Since the seekers initially lack proper understanding, they should place their faith in their sheikh.

The Ninth Treatise

On Maturity and Freedom

Chapter One

On the Meaning of Maturity and Freedom

(1)

Know that the community of dervishes asked of this beggar of God, Aziz O-Din Mohammad Nasafi to put together a writing regarding the nature of maturity and freedom.[1] May God assist me in what has been requested of me to avoid any errors.

(2)

Know that there is an end to all that exists, which comes with maturity and freedom. The Arabs say that some fruit reaches maturity and freedom when ripe enough to fall from the branch.

(3)

The end of something is when it reaches its beginnings. In this way, the circle completes itself. For example, to plant a seed and create the right conditions to ultimately bear a fruit whose seeds will give birth to the same fruit. The circle completes itself only when the seeds grow to bear the same fruit. The seed of the human being is the same way. This is the process through which maturity and freedom are obtained.

(4)
When the end comes and a person does not reach the beginning, it means that the circle has not completed itself, and that person remains incomplete. The gates of wisdom open only to those who understand and realize the secrets and subtleties of this.

(5)
Some have suggested that this seed is born from nature and returns to it. Others have said that this seed is born from Intelligence, or logos, to which it returns. Another group suggests that this seed comes from God and returns to Him in the end. It is our understanding that everything comes from God and then returns to God. It is through this journey from and to God that maturity and freedom are attained.

Chapter Two

On the Freedom and Maturity of Human Beings

(6)

Our philosophy is founded on the premise that the seed of all creation is Intelligence, or logos. The Prophet and Sufis have all stated that Intelligence was the first thing that was created by God. In that seed contained the root, the trunk, the branch, the leaf, and the fruit, which, upon falling, symbolizes maturity and freedom. The circle is complete! Creation springs forth from Intelligence and completes itself with the creation of human beings. Since there is nothing above them, they become the fruits of this tree of creation. Only when they attain maturity do they become complete. It is only at this stage that the circle completes itself.

(7)

O, dervish! Know that God created Intelligence, and there is nothing above that. Intelligence sits above all creation. Intelligence has many different levels, and no one attains Intelligence in its fullness. The final stage of Intelligence is divine light.

(8)

O, dervish! The circle completes itself for he who attains Intelligence. However, to achieve freedom, one must separate himself from the circle, very much like the fruit that separates itself from the branch that once held it.

(9)

O, dervish! Whatever existed, exists, and will exist is within this circle, for nothing can be outside of it. To be free is to be without desires, as desiring anything within the circle signifies attachment. And to be attached is to be a slave and not to be free.

(10)

O, dervish! To do things out of necessity is not the same thing as being a slave to them.

(12)

O, dervish! Those who say "We do not want old clothes but new ones" have superficial desires that enslave them. Free are those who have no attachments, for every attachment is like an idol that is worshipped. All idols[1] must be destroyed so that the heart remains empty and pure. God resides in such hearts.

(13)

O, dervish! Some idols come in the form of wealth, and others in the form of status and recognition.[2]

(14)

O, dervish! Do not engage in anything that harms another human being and never turn anything into a habit, for you become an idol worshipper. Whoever has an idol cannot speak of unity and freedom.

(15)

O, dervish! Know that it is possible to be wealthy, have a kingdom, and still be free. To experience no joy or sorrow in wealth and status and remain unaffected by the praise or the blame of the people. This is the meaning of maturity, contentment, surrender, and freedom.

The Tenth Treatise

On the Lesser World as a Representation of the Greater World

Chapter One

On the Greater and the Lesser Worlds

(1)

Know that the community of dervishes asked of this beggar of God, Aziz O-Din Mohammad Nasafi, to put together a work regarding the nature of the greater and the lesser worlds, for it has been said that the lesser world is a representation of the greater world. May God assist me in what has been requested of me to avoid any errors.

(2)

Upon creating the creation, God named it "the world." It is a sign of His existence, mercy, and power.

(3)

O, dervish! Creation is not only a sign but also a book. It has been said that whoever reads this book carefully shall come to know the wisdom, the mercy, and the power of God. The readers of the book were, at first, the angels. However, the book was so thick that they could not read it in its entirety. So the book was divided into two: the Greater World and the Lesser World. The first was the Great Book, and the second was called the Book of Intelligence, which contained the condensed version of the Great

Book. Hence anyone who read the Book of Intelligence was at the same time reading the Great Book. God then sent his deputy, Intelligence, into the lesser world before whom all the angels bowed. Then God created the human being who became the king in the Greater World and commanded all the angels to bow to this creation.[1] They all did except Satan.

(4)

O, dervish! In the Lesser World, God's deputy is Intelligence, and in the Greater World, it is the intelligence of the human being. Both worlds, however, represent the presence of God. When Intelligence is achieved, God's commandment, "Know yourself, your attributes and deeds so that you can come to know Me, My attributes and My deeds," is realized.

Chapter Two

On the Action of God and the Action of God's Deputy

(5)

Know that when God wants to create something, it first appears in God's Intelligence and then travels through the seven heavens and the light of the stars until it reaches this physical world. Nature, which is the king of this world, welcomes this new and invisible guest of God as it begins to manifest and reveal itself in this world. Hence creation exists in the Mind of God and then comes into physical existence through His command. And when it has served its purpose, it shall return to God.[1]

(6)

O, dervish! Now that you know God's actions in the Greater world, it would be beneficial to know His deputy's actions or deeds in the Lesser World. God's deputy in the Lesser World is Intelligence.

(7)

When God's deputy, Intelligence, wishes to do something, it first has its image in its mind and then makes it manifest in the Lesser World. The image and its manifestation become an act of God's deputy. In other words, Intelligence writes on nature and designs it accordingly.

(8)

O, dervish! Every art is first created within the mind's realm, after which it is expressed outwardly.

(10)

O, dervish! There were two words: *utterance* and *hearing*. The essences of the two words are rooted in God and came to be through His command. They are both God's deputies.

(11)

O, dervish! Like Adam, Jesus is a word that was uttered from the mouth of creation and entered the very essence of all things.

(12)

Hence know that whatever exists in the Greater World also exists in the Lesser World.

Chapter Four

On Adam and Eve

(14)

Know that just as there are Adam, Eve, angels, Satan, devils, beasts, and animals in the Greater World, so are they in the Lesser World.

(15)

O, dervish! Human beings are the Lesser World, and Intelligence is this world. The body is Eve, imagination is the devil, temptation is a peacock, anger is a serpent, noble manners are paradise, and evil manners are hell. And the powers of the intellect, spirit, and body are the angels.

(16)

O, dervish! Satan is one thing, and the devil is another. Satan is nature, and the devil is imagination.

(17)

O, dervish! Appearances, names, and attributes have no reality. What has reality is essence. A pig is not filthy because of its appearance but because of its greed and uncleanness. A dog is not filthy because of its appearance but because of its fierceness and viciousness. Thus when these qualities are also found in people, they are seen as dogs or pigs. Satan and the devil represent two entities that did not obey God. They were corrupt, jealous, and proud. So when such qualities are also found in human beings, they resemble Satan and the devil. An angel represents those who possess angelic attributes. God's deputy's task is to possess all the noble qualities and know the proper time and place to express each quality.[1]

(18)

O, dervish! The angel and the devil are the same force. When this force possesses people, they become either angels or devils. The task of God's deputies is not to annihilate them, for that is impossible, but to transform the forces from satanic to angelic. To tame the wild and give sight to the blind, to give understanding to the ignorant and give life to the dead. Those who manifest qualities possessed by dogs and pigs serve the devil and Satan and fulfill their desires. Such people shall remain poor and sick and servants to evil forces. Divine attributes disappear from them, and evil characteristics appear.

(19)

O, dervish! Those in whom God is absent resemble the devil or Satan, a dog or a pig. Even if they appear as human beings.

Chapter Five

On the Manifestation of Hell and Paradise

(20)

All the pleasures and comforts of paradise[1] and all pains and discomforts of hell exist in human beings.

(21)

Intelligence derives its pleasure from knowledge and wisdom. The physical body finds joy in food and comfort. The peace and comfort of those things that are heavenly are found in heavenly things, and the peace and comfort of worldly things are found in worldly things.

(22)

The body's desires are found in externalities, whereas the Intelligence desires inner things. Intelligence's peace and comfort lies in the fact that it can understand all creation's language and see God's wisdom in everything as well.

(23)

O, dervish! Everything in creation speaks of God's wisdom to those who possess Intelligence, and herein lies their comfort and peace, for everywhere they turn, they see God and are in the presence of God. This peace and comfort are of a certain quality such that not a trace of regret or sorrow can be found in them.

The Eleventh Treatise

On Earthly, Heavenly, and Celestial (Intelligent) Realms

Chapter One

On the World

(1)

Know that the community of dervishes asked of this beggar of God, Aziz O-Din Mohammad Nasafi, to put together a work regarding the nature of earthly, heavenly, and celestial realms. May God assist me in what has been requested of me to avoid any errors.

(3)

The world consists of the visible and invisible realms, or the sensible and the intelligible worlds. These two realms have been given different names: the created world and the commanded world, the manifest world and the unmanifested world, the dark world and the illuminated world.

(4)

O, dervish! The earthly, heavenly, and celestial are three different worlds, and they all belong to God. The celestial realm, however, does not have an external existence. The three worlds are not separate from each other but exist within one another. The celestial kingdom is the essence or the root from which the two different realms come into existence.

(5)

O, dervish! Whatever has come to be in this world or the heavenly one first existed in the celestial realm. That is, their existence is rooted in the invisible world.[1]

(6)

The Lesser World reflects the Greater World, and thus everything in the Lesser World also exists in the Greater World.

(7)

Know that the seed that creates human beings exists in the celestial realm. Their bodies and souls, however, belong to the earthly and heavenly realms. Hence their bodies and souls were hidden in the seed and became visible in the heavenly and earthly realms.

(8)

O, dervish! Whatever exists in the Greater World also exists in the Lesser World. It can also be said the essence is the seed, the body and the soul are the tree, and the deeds or actions are the fruits.

(9)

The point is that all existence is one being, and the physical, heavenly, and celestial or intelligible planes are merely different levels of existence. Furthermore, whatever name you wish to assign this being is acceptable, and should no name be assigned to it, that is fine as well.

Chapter Two

A Further Discussion of the Physical, Heavenly, and Intelligible Realms

(17)

O, dervish! A celestial person is different than a heavenly one, and a physical person is different from an earthly one. The celestial person resides at the highest level of creation. The celestial realm is the cause of all creation. The heavenly person lives at the highest heavenly plane, the kingdom of Intelligence—the first thing to be created in this plane. The physical person resides at the highest plane of physical existence. The earthly person reflects all wisdom and divine light. Such a person is called the perfected being.[1] All wisdom and knowledge originate from such a being.

(18)

O, dervish! Light descended upon human beings and transformed them into itself—light.

(19)

The celestial realm desired a mirror so that it could see and experience its nature and attributes. So it created the physical world, and in the creation of the physical world, two elements came into being: light and darkness. Darkness, however, is the companion and protector of light.

(21)

O, dervish! Know that the ocean of light exists in the angelic realm, and the sea of darkness is the physical realm. This ocean of light and water of life, which exists in the sea of darkness, can only be attained by traveling through this ocean of darkness.

(22)

O, dervish! You have heard that the water of life is in the darkest realms, yet you do not know where the water of life or the darkest realms are. Some seekers have reached and seen the infinite ocean of light. It is because of this light that there is life, knowledge, and wisdom. It is because of this light that there is hearing, seeing, and speaking. It is because of this light that creatures have their respective natures and attributes. All are the manifestation of this light. Everything is light, and the sea of darkness is the protector of this light.

(23)

This ocean of light is the seven realms, or the father, and this sea of darkness is called the mother, who holds water, air, earth, and fire. These two have embraced one another to create such things as vegetables, animals, and humans. The fruits of creation are nothing more than this. They appear from nowhere and disappear to nowhere. From one, they become many, and from many, they become one. The wisdom of coming together is so that they can ascend to perfection and mirror creation. In this way, the ocean of light and the sea of darkness can see themselves, their nature, and their attributes.

Chapter Five

On Advice

(28)

Know that the desires of the wise person are always for the sake of tranquility and unity.[1] In this way, they shall distance themselves from fragmentation and sorrow. Unity, harmony, and tranquility then are three of the most profound blessings bestowed to such persons.

(29)

O, dervish! Become a seeker of unity, harmony, and tranquility and distance yourself from things that cause you fragmentation, pain, and sorrow. Know that unity, harmony, and tranquility cannot be found in status and wealth. They are the cause of fragmentation, pain, and sorrow. Unity, harmony, and tranquility, and certainty can all be found and experienced in the presence of a wise person.

The Twelfth Treatise

On Heavenly, Angelic, and Physical Realms: Part One

Chapter One

On the Nature of the Heavenly Realm

(1)

O, dervish! This treatise regarding the heavenly and angelic realms is essential to dervishes.

(2)

Know that the physical plane is the realm of manifestation and thus is the sensible world. The angelic realm is the invisible realm and is the intelligible world. And the heavenly realm is the plane of essence where things are created.[1]

(3)

O, dervish! The heavenly realm is the ultimate reality, which is unfathomable.

(4)

O, dervish! Every created thing is designed for a specific task and cannot do a task for which it was not made. The fox can never become a sheep, and the sheep can never become a fox. All created things follow this design.

(5)

O, dervish! There are specific attributes within the nature of a fox, and the same is true with a sheep. They are born with their unique character. However, people's physical and spiritual natures are designed for change and transformation, which is the reason for the teachings of the prophets and saints—so that they can transform. The character of some people resembles a fox, whereas others' natures resemble a sheep. A wild fox runs away from people, whereas a sheep is attracted to people. People's essence will always remain the same, but their character has the potential to change.

(6)

O, dervish! The essence of the human being remains unchanged, but their attributes can change.

Chapter Two

On Being, Nonbeing, and Love

(7)

Know that the essence of the things that descend from the celestial plane to the physical plane will once again return to the celestial realm and will cease to exist after that.

(9)

Anything that exists in the world of being has its essence in the celestial realm.

(10)

O, dervish! The journey from the world of being to the world of nonbeing is not too long, and the difference between the two is not too significant. Both worlds are tightly connected. One merely is more abstract than the other. The world of nonbeing is a book, and the world of being is the design imprinted on the book. Every few days, a caravan travels from the world of nonbeing into this world of being, stays for some time, and then travels back to the world of nonbeing.

(11)

O, dervish! God has many treasures in the world of nonbeing, such as wealth and status, shelter and security, knowledge and creativity, and separation and union.

(12)

O, dervish! The five senses can take one to the physical plane, but not the celestial realm. The mind may take you to the angelic realm but finds itself perplexed and bewildered in its presence. However, love[1] takes you to the celestial kingdom, for this is the realm of love, and all things in this realm exist in love itself, which desires a mirror into which it can look and see itself. The physical plane is the mirror of the celestial kingdom.

(13)

O, dervish! All stages of being and nonbeing are filled with love. The entire existence is consumed with love. When the seekers reach the stage of love, they are burnt, cleansed, and completely purified with the fire of love. In this way, they become like the community of the celestial plane. The seekers' hearts become mirrors into which they can gaze and come to know and understand the celestial plane. They shall come to know what shall manifest in this realm before it is manifested. What others may see in their dreams, they shall witness in wakefulness.

(14)

O, dervish! That seeing is not possible with the eyes of the head but with the eye of the heart.[2] When the seekers reach the stage of love, their hearts' mirrors become so clear, cleansed, and purified that the entire universe is revealed to them. Whatever flows from the ocean of the celestial realm to the shore of the manifested realm, whatever flows from the ocean of the celestial kingdom shall be known to them before it reaches the shore of the physical realm.

(15)

O, dervish! There is a community whose hearts are so pure that they receive revelations. Some animals are known to have such receptivity. Whatever misfortunes or blessings to come to this world are known by these animals, which try to communicate them to people. But only some will understand the messages that the animals are trying to convey.

(17)

O, dervish! The ability to perceive the unseen has nothing to do with being religious or irreligious, or wise or ignorant, but in possessing a pure heart. This ability is then possible for both the perfect and the imperfect beings, the righteous and the sinner. The purehearted are a blessing to everyone. Those who are evil are the cause of suffering and sorrow for many.

Chapter Three

On Advice

(19)

Know that the state of this world will never remain constant. It is always changing and is in a continual state of flux. Every moment has a birth and a death of a created thing.[1]

(20)

O, dervish! Know that the world does not remain in one state but is in a constant state of flux. It resembles the waves of the sea or is, in fact, the sea itself. The wise never build anything on either the waves or the sea itself. Know for sure that we are but travelers in this world, and the various things and states of the world are nothing but travelers. And whether these states are pleasant, rest assured that they will pass. Therefore, whether your state is a pleasant or a sorrowful one, do not become consumed by it. Become neither joyous nor sad, as you do not yet know what the next hour will bring. Be concerned with only two things: serving others and doing them as little harm as possible.

The Thirteenth Treatise

On the Celestial, Angelic, and Physical Realms: Part Two

Chapter One

On Unity

(1)

Know that the community of dervishes asked of this beggar of God, Aziz O-Din Mohammad Nasafi, to put together a work regarding the exterior and interior makeup of human beings. That is, to discuss the evolution and the purpose of the soul. May God assist me in what has been requested of me to avoid any errors.

(2)

Know that the physical realm is the place of multiplicity, the angelic realm is the place of singularity and individuality, and the celestial kingdom is the place of unity. There is neither multiplicity nor singularity in the celestial sphere; it is a place of unity. It contains everything and nothing.

(3)

O, dervish! The realm of essence is very much the same, as it contains everything and nothing simultaneously. The celestial realm is uncontaminated and pure. It is nameless, shapeless, and formless. In the angelic realm, however, forms and shapes appear with names and attributes. It is where spiritual and angelic entities come into being. The physical realm is a place of multiplicity where the elements of fire, water, earth, and wind were created.

It is a sphere of past, present, and future or yesterday, today, and tomorrow.

(4)

O, dervish! In the celestial realm, poison and its antidote are grown in the same place, and the fox and sheep live together. In the celestial realm, day and night and light and darkness all have the same color, and yesterday, today, tomorrow, and eternity are all one thing. Satan is no longer the enemy, and the Pharaoh no longer quarrels with Moses.

(5)

O, dervish! There is unity before multiplicity, and there is unity after multiplicity, and if the seekers attain the latter form of unity, they shall become freed of multiplicity.[1]

(6)

O, dervish! If there were no multiplicity, there would have been no unity, for unity brings together the many. And there are two ways to unite the many: either through knowledge or through action. There are, therefore, two forms: unity of knowledge and unity of action.

(7)

O, dervish! Those who have attained the ultimate unity cannot but see Nimrod and Abraham or Moses and the Pharaoh as one and the same—even if they are fighting with one another. This is the ultimate stage of unity.

Chapter Two

On the Night of Revelation

(8)

Know that the physical and the angelic realms are the attributes of the celestial realm. Anything that is hidden in the celestial realm is revealed in the angelic and the physical realms.

(9)

O, dervish! The angelic realm is the manifestation of the celestial realm, and the physical realm is the manifestation of the angelic realm. In this way, the physical realm will ascend to the angelic realm, and the angelic realm will ascend to the celestial realm. The angelic realm is the mirror of the celestial realm, and the physical realm is the mirror of the angelic realm. The angelic realm can see itself in the physical realm, and the celestial realm can see itself in the angelic realm. Therefore, it was said, whatever was hidden in the celestial realm was revealed. This is what is meant by the "Night of Revelation."[1]

Chapter Three

On Advice

(11)

Know that within the mind of all human beings is the desire to be a king, a ruler, or a sheikh. Everyone has one of these three desires. Wise are those who continually try to annihilate these desires from their minds. The desire for status is the last thing that the wise must remove from their minds and hearts. The rest of humanity is a slave to this desire and must burn in the hell that this desire creates. It is human nature to think of oneself as unique and unmatched in intelligence and character. Hence one always sees oneself above everybody else. This community suffers from arrogance and pride and desires to be praised by others day and night and laments if the praise goes to someone else.

(12)

O, dervish! Suffering, arrogance, and pride will always reside where there is a lack of intelligence and wisdom. And where there is wisdom and intelligence, such traits will never make their presence known.

(13)

O, dervish! Know that no one can know and do everything. The universe's order consists of all created things in their proper stage of being and existence. Hence in whatever stage you are, it is a stage that has been designated to you in the realm of existence. Since the wise have become aware of this truth, they chose to be in a stage within the stages of existence where there is less sorrow, suffering, and fragmentation and more union and contemplation.

(14)

O, dervish! The universe has placed you in a specific stage of existence. Be content with your position and what has been put in your lot. Spend your time in contemplation and union and try with all your might not to cause injury or harm to another, for there is no sin greater than injuring another human being. Be the cause of solace and comfort for others and not misery. Know that whatever anyone does, whether good or evil, they do it to themselves, and they will be either rewarded or punished for what they have done. This is the natural law.

The Twenty-Second Treatise

On Heaven and Hell

Chapter One

On Heaven and Hell and Adam and Eve

(1)

Know that the community of dervishes asked of this beggar of God, Aziz O-Din Mohammad Nasafi, to put together a work regarding the true nature of heaven and hell and the true nature of joy and sorrow. Also, to discuss the many heavens and hells that exist and explain which tree caused Adam and Eve[1] to be thrown out of paradise. May God assist me in what has been requested of me to avoid any errors.

(2)

O, dervish! The famous tale of Adam and Eve and heaven and hell has always existed but know that inwardly we have an Adam and an Eve, a heaven and a hell.

(3)

Know that paradise's true nature is affirmation, and the true nature of hell is denial, and the true nature of joy is coming into union with that which is sought, and the true nature of sorrow is being separated from that which is being sought. Now know that there are many gates to heaven and hell. The good and the pure-intentioned words and deeds represent the gates of heaven, and the bad and the ill-intentioned words and deeds represent the gates of hell. Every joy or sorrow that visits man comes either from good and pure-intentioned words and deeds or their opposite.

Chapter Two

On the Gates of Heaven and Hell

(4)

Know that some say that the gates of hell are seven and the gates of heaven are eight. Understanding is achieved in eight different ways: the five senses, vision, imagination, and intelligence. When understanding comes from the first seven gates (five senses, vision, and imagination) and lacks intelligence, they lead one to hell.[1] But when intelligence appears and begins to govern these seven gates, all eight gates lead to heaven. Hence all people must first enter hell to reach heaven. Of course, some will remain in hell without exiting it, and some will enter it and then go towards heaven.

(5)

O, dervish! Most people shall remain in hell without the ability to pass through it.

Chapter Three

On the Stages of Heaven and Hell

(7)

Know that there are different stages of heaven and hell. The seeker's perception of heaven and hell is different from the ordinary person's, and the lover's perception of heaven and hell is different from the learned's. The heaven and hell of the arrogant lie in their acceptance and rejection. The heaven and hell of the learned lie in attachment and detachment, and the heaven and hell of the lover lie in that which is veiled or revealed.

(8)

O, dervish! Love is a fire, and when it enters the seekers' hearts, all their attachments, alien thoughts, and idols disappear. It is here that the seekers become cleansed and purified.

(9)

O, dervish! Love is Moses's staff, and the world is the magician that lures people into its deceptive illusions. The world deceives people into taking illusions as reality. However, when love opens its mouth, it swallows the world as a whole and purifies the seeker. It is here that the seeker's name becomes "the purified one." Such a person can now be called a Sufi.

(10)

O, dervish! The seeker must journey through various stages before attaining the stage of Sufism and being given the name Sufi. The Sufi must journey through various stages before attaining the stage of wisdom and given the name Gnostic. And the Gnostic must journey through various stages until coming to the stage of holiness to be named Guardian, Master, Lord, Protector, or Sheikh. Sufism, whose end is guardianship, is a profound position and not many seekers rise to that position.

(11)

O, dervish! So long as the stage of love has not been reached, the mind is the seekers' staff or helper. The mind is usually busy with the world, which is without love and thus lifeless. And that which is lifeless is dead.

(12)

O, dervish! Let go of the mind, for it is occupied with worldly affairs. This is destructive to you. Instead, turn your mind towards us, the Sufis! The seekers cannot let go of the mind on their own; only love can assist them on this matter. Upon love's arrival, the mind will depart.

(13)

O, dervish! Without divine light, the darkness of the world cannot be seen. Whoever turns towards the world turns towards desires and destruction. The mind resembles a snake that creates fear and illusions. It makes you a slave and keeps you from the Path. Do not be fearful of this snake. Make it your slave so that it can assist you in your journey towards God.

(14)

O, dervish! All creation refused to keep a secret that was given to human beings. They accepted that treasure, which was love. However, if they knew what a difficult task love is and what hardship they must endure and misfortunes they shall experience because of love, they would have never accepted it.[1]

Notes

Introduction

1 *Maghsad al-ghasee* (The sublime destination) is a collection of Aziz O-Din Nasafi's thoughts on God's essence and attributes, the friends and prophets of God, and various levels of existence.

Introductory Treatise

Chapter One. The Law, the Way, and the Truth

1 *Dervish* is a Persian word. Traditionally, someone who abstains from worldly desires and has chosen a life of inner simplicity is given such a title.

2 In the Sufi tradition, *faqir*, or "beggar," is a specific inner emptiness or poverty that can only be filled or nourished by God.

3 *Salik*, or "seeker," refers to someone who has been initiated into the Sufi path and is ready to receive instructions.

4 The three principles that sum up the entire Sufi tradition are *Shariat*, or "the Law"; *Tarighat*, or "the Way"; and *Haghighat*, or "the Truth." The Law can be viewed as a set of specific teachings or instructions given to the seeker or the pupil by their teacher or sheikh. The Way refers to the Path or, more correctly, how the teachings should be applied. The teachings' application has intense physical, emotional, psychological, intellectual, and spiritual effects that the teacher needs to oversee. The instructions and their application are designed to create the proper physical, emotional, psychological, intellectual, and spiritual conditions so that the student can become worthy of glimpses of Truth.

Chapter Two. On the Perfect Being

1 *Sheikh* is a Muslim spiritual teacher or a Sufi master.

2 *Khizr* is a Quranic figure who serves God by teaching and giving special mystical knowledge to prophets, saints, and sages.

3 It is a stage of being where the only poverty that exists is not being in the presence of God. This form of poverty, according to Sufism, liberates the seeker from the physical world and its occupants. His is an important note, as it illustrates the absence of any desires that relate to the physical world. It is important to note that this specific kind of inner poverty requires specific instructions and training given from the Sufi teacher to his pupil. Also, being an antidote to pride and egoism, poverty allows for the presence of humility and selflessness.

Chapter Three. On Perfect Freedom

1 There are two stages to *khalvat*, or "solitude." The first is the beginner's stage on the Path, which requires the seeker to physically avoid any social environment that can distract one's focus and attention from the Path. This, in the Sufi Naghsh-bandi Order that was formed in the fourteenth century, is called *yad bood*, or "remembrance." That is, the seeker must always remember the Path and never forget or deviate from it. The second stage is called *khalvat dar anjoman*, or "solitude in the crowd." This stage is where the seeker is fully involved in family and social life while, at the same time, sees and experiences God's presence in all activities.

2 *Reza*, or "contentment," is a stage where the seeker is satisfied with whatever God places in their life.

Chapter Four. On Speech

1 According to the Sufi tradition, speech falls into different stages, each expressing the seeker's emotional, intellectual, and spiritual stage. The first stage is chatter or unreflective speech. Next is reflective speech. This contains emotions of curiosity and interest. However, it lacks proper understanding. Next is one in which the seeker has established a strong and intense relationship with the guide and the Path. At this

point, there exists a fair amount of longing and yearning in the seeker's speech. This is usually called the speech of the heart. The next stage is when speech moves into a stage of silence. That is when the seeker is fully aware that words cannot adequately convey the longing of one's heart. As the seeker moves into the next stage, speech contains understanding and heart. The final stage is when the seeker becomes a messenger and speaks only when there is a message to convey.

2 *Adab*, or "manners," in the Sufi tradition refers to one's physical conduct in the presence of the guide, other seekers, God, and other people.

Chapter Five. On the Journey

1 In the Sufi tradition, those who are on the spiritual path go through three phases. The first is journeying toward God. This requires the complete annihilation of one's physical, emotional, psychological, and intellectual history. It must once again be emphasized that in the Sufi tradition, this first stage is impossible to do on one's own and a guide is necessary. The next stage is journeying in God—that is, experiencing, understanding, and applying His attributes, such as mercy, compassion, justice and beauty. And finally, the seeker must become worthy of God journeying in them.

2 The Arabic word is *fana fi-lah* or "annihilation in God." Such persons who have achieved this are called "God-intoxicated."

3 This is a pantheistic idea that everything, in some shape or form, has a spark of God in it.

Chapter Twelve. On the Evolution of the Human Spirit

1 The Persian word is *Ahl Ma'arefat*; these are those who possess mystical or spiritual knowledge and wisdom.

Chapter Thirteen. On the Number of Souls

1 *Ghabz*, or "contraction," refers to a state in which the seeker is suddenly gripped with sorrow, longing, and the feeling of being spiritually abandoned.

2 *Bast*, or "expansion," refers to a state in which the seeker suddenly feels union with God and, with it, a sense of wholeness and perfection.

Chapter Fifteen. On Advice

1 In the Sufi tradition, the heart must be reserved for God alone. It must remain pure and vacant to receive God's presence.

2 Islam does not believe in or encourage monastic life. Seekers are encouraged to be wholly devoted to the spiritual path as well as social life and activities.

The Second Treatise

Chapter One. On the Essence of Being

1 There are three forms of knowledge in the Sufi tradition. The first is *eyn-ul yaghin*, or "knowledge through the senses." Then there is *ilm-ul yaghin*, or "intellectual knowledge." Lastly, there is *hagh-ul yaghin*, or "divine knowledge."

2 These are the three stages of spiritual maturity that the seeker must journey through. All seekers are initially imitators, as they must blindly follow the instructions of their guide. Once they graduate from the first stage, they begin journeying through the next stage by reflecting upon their guide's instructions. The final stage consists of the seeker no longer being interested in imitation or reflection but patiently awaiting God's revelation.

Chapter Two. On the Community of Imitators: The Common Person

1 This refers to the following passages in the Islamic sacred text, the Quran: "Those who utter God's qualities with their tongue will be tested and be brought to shame before God" (29:2–3); "Your tongues moved and your mouths spoke of something of which you had no knowledge. You thought it to be a trivial matter, while in the eyes of God it is blasphemy" (24:15).

2 "Al-baghara" (The cow), the second and the longest chapter in the Quran, contains many passages regarding the pain and sorrow that

are visited upon those whose lives are only governed by sensory experiences.

Chapter Three. On the Uniqueness of the Community of Intellectuals

1 The concept of intellectuality here should not be mistaken for that of the eighteenth-century in the Western world's Age of Reason, which ultimately birthed secularism and capitalism. Intellectuality in Sufism is the conceptual and experiential expression of one's encounter with certain attributes of God.

2 In the Sufi tradition, the guide can only create the proper physical, emotional, intellectual, and spiritual environment for the seeker so that certain divine experiences can become possible.

Chapter Four. On the Community of Revelation

1 This is a stage where one intellectually knows and understands that all that takes place is ultimately willed by God and is moving toward Him.

2 *Yad bood*, or "remembrance," is a stage in which the seeker must remember and be aware of God's presence in thought, speech, and action.

3 *Al-Rahman* and *Al-Rahim*—"compassion" and "mercy"—have profound significance in Sufi thought. Compassion, which is a feminine attribute, has a giving function. However, without proper education, that which has been given will not be used and applied properly. Mercy, which is a masculine attribute, is a judgment upon how that which was given was applied.

4 The word *education* is derived from the Latin *educatio*, which means "to bring up" or "to bring out." For ancient Greek philosophers such as Plato and Aristotle, education was designed to lead the person toward happiness, fulfillment, or flourishing. Education, for the Sufis as well, has to do with training the physical, emotional, intellectual, and spiritual bodies of the human being properly to become worthy of God's presence.

Chapter Five. Another Community within the Community of Unity

1 Chapter 112 of the Quran speaks about God's oneness and the non-existence of anything else except God.

2 *Khi'yal*, or "imagination," which was one of the key philosophical concepts of the twelfth-century Sufi Ibn al-Arabi, here suggests that the world as it appears to human beings exists only within the realm of human imagination. It is both an aspect of God (*wajh*) as well as a veil (*hijab*). It is real and unreal or unseen (*ghayb*) as well as visible (*shahadat*).

The Third Treatise

Chapter One. On Three Groups of Human Beings, Who Are a Mixture of Material and Spiritual

1 There are three different types of ego. The first is *nafs al-ammārah*, where all human actions lack reflection and frequently cause harm to oneself and others. The second is called *nafs al-lawwāmah*, where there is much reflection and often actions that have negative consequences and cause profound shame and guilt. Lastly is *nafs al-mutmainnah*, where the ego is so refined and consumed by God's presence that all actions are a blessing to oneself and others.

2 The great Sufi poet Attar, in his work *Tazkeratol oleeya* (Conference of the birds), states that the seeker must journey through the "Seven Valleys," each of which creates a different physical, emotional, intellectual, and spiritual state that help refine the human ego and ready it to experience a specific aspect of God. The first is the Valley of *Quest*, the second is the Valley of *Love*, the third is the Valley of *Inner Knowledge*, the fourth is the Valley of *Detachment*, the fifth is the Valley of *Awe*, and, finally, last is the Valley of *Poverty*.

Chapter Five. On the Placement of Spirits

1 *Zahir*, or appearance, is a stage where the person is governed by the six senses. The first five senses (sight, hearing, smell, touch, and taste) allow for the physical body and to interact with the physical world. The sixth sense is memory, which holds and stores all experiences.

2 There are three different categories of human beings in the Sufi tradition, inferred from the Quran. The first category is *En'son*, which means "forgetful." Those in this category are gripped by their sense perceptions and derive their pleasure from them. The next category of human being is *Bashar*, which means "desiring to become noble." Those in this category have had specific nonsensory experiences. However, they keep bouncing back and forth between forgetfulness and awareness. This, in Sufism, is considered *barzakh*, which is equivalent to purgatory. *Adam* is the final category. It represents the perfected human being in the Sufi tradition.

Chapter Six. On the Soul's Fate

1 There is a tale in the Quran, in chapter "Kahf" (The cave), that speaks of the definite capacity of each soul. In the story, Moses demands that God grant him more insight into the mysteries of life, but God tells him that he does not have the capacity for his request. Only after being tested three times and having failed three times is Moses' spiritual greed tamed, and he becomes content with his capacity.

Chapter Seven. On God's Destiny

1 *Tajali*, or "manifestation," in Sufism is the idea that the physical world's entire content symbolizes God's presence. The knowing of this can range from the most basic and superficial to the most profound and transformational, from merely physical to imitational, emotional, intellectual, and finally, spiritual. Only through proper training can a spiritual knowing of this be attained and experienced. The *zikr*, or Sufi chant "La ilaha illal-lah," affirms that God's presence is everywhere and in everything.

Chapter Nine. On Human Beings, in Whom Are Contained Both This and the Other World

1 According to the Sufis, the human being has two responsibilities: ascension and descension. They must ascend toward God, and once

they reach Him, they must descend to educate and care for God's creation.

The Fourth Treatise

Chapter One. On the Creation and Resurrection according to the Community of Wisdom

1 There is a tale in the Sufi tradition that God desired to reveal Himself to His creation. He revealed Himself to the mountains, but they shattered into pieces. Next, He revealed Himself to the oceans, but they quickly dried up. He tried all His creation, but none could endure His presence. He finally revealed Himself to the human being, and to His surprise, the human-animal was able to house Him. However, knowing man's nature and how potentially corrupt he could become, God hid Himself in the deepest part of the human being. Then He turned to all of creation, including the angles, and commanded them to bow to the human being, for within them lies the potential for *absolute perfection.*

Chapter Two. On the Intelligence and Structure of the Lower World

1 According to the Sufi tradition, every physical and spiritual life falls within the domain of *ghesmat*, or "destiny," which is in God's hands and therefore willed by Him.

Chapter Three. On Resurrection

1 In Sufi tradition, upon death, the soul sits near the body that housed it for three days and contemplates all the deceased's physical, emotional, and intellectual activities while alive. Once all actions have been recorded, the soul journeys to God and awaits His judgment.

Chapter Four. On the State of the Soul after Its Release from the Body

1 Islam, like Judaism and Christianity, is a linear religion. All three believe that life begins and expires at certain points. Judaism did not

initially have the concepts of the soul, hell or heaven, and Judgment Day. Only after its encounter with the Persian religion Zoroastrianism were those concepts adopted into its theology. The idea of reincarnation does not exist in any of the three religions. Many scholars have argued that since the idea of reincarnation cannot be found in Mohammad's teachings or the Quran, it must have been adopted from some of the Eastern religious traditions, such as Hinduism and Buddhism.

Chapter Five. On Advice

1 *Nafs al-ammārah*, or "lower self," is entirely sensory driven. Reflection, shame, guilt, and remorse, all of which could have a baptizing quality, are, for the most part, absent. In the language of the Greek philosopher Plato, who in the Sufi tradition is considered the Master of Illumination, this self exists in the cave and takes the shadow and the mirages as real.

The Fifth Treatise

Chapter One. On Traversing the Path

1 There are three stages in the Sufi path. The first stage is the journey to God. In this stage, many habits and assumptions about oneself, others, the concepts of right and wrong, and God must be removed. All this must take place under the direct supervision of one's guide. Once purity of body, mind, and heart are attained, the seeker enters the stage of *sabr*, or "patience." Here, the seeker must wait until God reveals certain aspects of Himself to them. This is called a journey in God. The final stage, which is rarely reached, is when God begins His journey in the seeker to experience Himself.

2 Sufis believe that since human beings are created in God's image, then the more self-knowledge one has, the closer one comes to knowing and understanding God.

Chapter Two. On the Intention of the Seeker on the Path

1 I will translate one of most profound illustrations of how maturity is obtained in the Sufi tradition, a tale told by Attar in his book

Tazkeratol oleeya (Conference of the birds), originally told by the great Persian Sufi of the eleventh century Abu Saeed Abul-Khayr. It is reported that a wealthy young man by chance passed a lecture hall where Abu Saeed was giving a sermon. He became so captivated by what he heard that he decided to give all his possessions to the sheikh to be distributed among the poor.

Accepting him, Abu Saeed commanded the young man to pray and fast for a few months while also giving him the task of cleaning the bathhouse for a year. After the year was over, he was instructed to care for the needs of the kitchen and the dervishes.

After some time, the sheikh went to the town and prohibited the people from giving the young man anything and told them not to pay him any attention. Such an environment was created that the only person that the young man could turn to was Abu Saeed. But after some time had passed, even Abu Saeed began to treat him harshly, both in words and in deeds, in private and in public.

Abu Saeed instructed his disciples to abstain from giving the young man any food and to deliberately make things difficult for him. On the fourth day, Abu Saeed instructed his disciples to not allow the young man to enter the *khaneghah*, the gathering place of the Sufis. The young man arrived at the *khaneghah* with an empty basket, tired, hungry, and thirsty. But he was not allowed in. After much begging, the sheikh turned to him and shouted, "You miserable and wretched fool, why do you not look for work so that you can feed yourself?" He was pushed around by the disciples and then kicked out. Having lost all hope in people, his friends, and his master, the young man went to a mosque in utter exhaustion and desperation. While weeping, he raised his arms toward the heavens and said, "O, God! You have seen how I have been treated. No one accepts me, and I have no one to turn to except You." As he lay on the floor weeping, suddenly God revealed Himself to the young man.

The sheikh, of course, aware of young man's illumination, instructed his disciples to each take a candle and walk toward the mosque. When they reached the mosque, the young man turned to the sheikh and said, "O, Abu Saeed, why did you treat me in such a manner?"

The sheikh replied, "You must now share your illumination with us all."

"But tell me why," asked the young man, "was I treated in such a way?"

"O, child!" responded Abu Saeed. "You had to abandon all hope in people, and the condition for that had to be created. Then the only veil that remained between you and God was Abu Saeed. So I removed myself by behaving in a crude manner towards you. Now rise, for you have been illuminated. It is time to be joyous. Such is the way of this Path."

2 I will translate a well-known old Persian satirical tale that speaks of the enormous difficulty of the inner quest in which a man has lost the key to his house and is looking for it on the ground outside. As it happens, a friend passes by and inquires as to what the man is doing. Upon hearing the man's dilemma, the friend decides to help look for the lost key.

After an exhaustive search, the friend asks, "Where do you think you lost the key?"

"Inside the house," replies the man.

The bewildered friend asks, "If the key was lost inside the house, why are you looking for it outside?"

"Because," says the man, "there is more light out here."

Chapter Three. On the Attainment of Wisdom through the Purification of the Body

1 There are three jewels in Zoroastrianism: right thinking, right speech, and right conduct. Zoroaster believed that it would take many years to train an individual to think correctly. Once thinking was morphed into wisdom, it would then take many more years of training to put wisdom into a linguistic container. This would prove enormously difficult, as words reveal themselves to be unfit vehicles for wisdom. Once there was a harmonious relationship between wisdom

and language, they both would enter a new stage: action. This last stage would ultimately refine wisdom and language and ready them for practical application.

Chapter Four. On the Three Groups of People

1 "Allah does hold a soul responsible beyond its capacity. Every soul will only bear the consequences of its actions. Allah will not impose blame if we forget or make a mistake. Our Lord! Do not make us bear a burden for which we have no strength. And pardon us, and grant us forgiveness, and have mercy on us" (Quran 2:286).

Chapter Five. On the Path to the Destination

1 In Sufism, the seeker journeys through two forms of submission. The first is that they must completely submit to the sheikh. Translating from the Persian, the twelfth-century Persian Sufi poet Hafez states, "Soak the prayer rug with wine should the sheikh demand of you; the seeker is unaware of the path and the ways to the Destination." Hafez is pointing out that at times, the Sufi guide will demand that the seeker take specific actions that are contrary to the teachings of the Quran and Prophet Mohammad and disrespectful to cultural and social etiquette. Yet the seeker must do what is asked of them without question. The second form of submission is to the will of God. That is, the seeker must perceive how every aspect of their life is willed by God and must accept it joyfully.

Chapter Six. On the Level of the Common Person

1 This chapter refers to the inner and outer teachings of Islam. Some only have the capacity to be guided by the exoteric, outer and literal aspect of Islam, whereas others have the capacity to be given the inner, esoteric aspect of the tradition. The latter are the Sufis.

Chapter Seven. On the Conditions of the Journey

1 Islamic tradition holds an annual fasting month called Ramezan or Seeyum, where the observant abstain from eating, drinking, and

smoking from sunrise to sunset. This month of fasting can last anywhere from twenty-eight to thirty-one days. In Arabic, the word *ramezan* comes from the word *ramez*, a baby camel or calf. In Sufism, the seekers are often likened to camels because of what they must endure on the spiritual journey. Camels are generally in the desert's scorching sun and travel without food and water in the harshest and driest of places. That is what the seekers must endure as they physically, emotionally, and intellectually divorce themselves from all things physical, emotional, and intellectual and live in a metaphoric desert. The other name for this fasting month is Seeyum, or silence. The Sufis believe this is one of God's names, and thus there is no month in which it begins or ends. This becomes symbolic of silencing the physical, emotional, intellectual desires of the lower-self, or *nafs al-ammārah*.

Chapter Eight. The Pillars of the Path

1 Khizr is the servant of God whose symbolic color is green—means life, peace, and submission—and who bestows wisdom to those who are worthy to receive it.

Chapter Nine. On Veils and Status

1 There are five pillars in the Islamic tradition: *shahdat*, or the confession that only one God and Mohammad is His messenger; *salat*, or prayer; *zekat*, or almsgiving; *ramezan*, or fasting; *hajj*, or pilgrimage to Mecca, the house of God.

2 A branch on Sufism called Malamati, or "the Path of Blame," was born in the ninth century, Its core philosophy was that any desire, goal, pleasure, and joy rooted in the lower-self, *nafs al-ammārah*, must be annihilated. The task is to purify one's body, mind, and emotions so that one can become worthy of God's presence.

Chapter Ten. On Training

1 One of the best accounts of Sufi training can be found in the book *Daughter of Fire* by Irina Tweedie. At almost a thousand pages, it is a

diary that charts her spiritual journey. The book provides many helpful insights especially for the modern reader regarding one of the most critical aspects of the Sufi tradition: the student-teacher relationship.

The Sixth Treatise: On the Manners of Solitude

Chapter One. On Obedience and Disobedience

1 The number forty is significant and sacred in many religious-spiritual traditions. In Sufism, it signifies completion. This training is designed to create extremely intense physical, emotional, intellectual, and spiritual states for the seeker. Alone and in the dark, the seeker must sit for forty days and forty nights. The nights and days are spent in prayer and fasting.

Chapter Two. On the Conditions of the Forty Days' Training

1 The chant's purpose is to have the words reach an intense emotional climax so that they can penetrate the heart to achieve an intimacy and union between the seeker and God.

*Chapter Three. On the Manners of Remembrance of God (*Zikr*)*

1 This is a reference to the Ka'aba in Mecca, Saudi Arabia, the most sacred place of worship in the Islamic tradition. Originally in the ancient city of Ur (in present-day Iraq), it housed 365 idols of worship, most of which were sculpted by Abraham's father, Azar. Abraham, in the Islamic tradition, destroyed all the idols to illustrate to his community the powerlessness and the incompetence of the gods. For the Sufis, the Ka'aba represents the human heart, which is filled with desires or idols of worship. It is the task of the sheikh to cleanse the seeker's heart of all that is impure.

Chapter Four. On the Ascent of the Sufis

1 There are, in the Sufi tradition, three kinds of certainty. The first is *eyn-ul yaghin*, or "certainty through the five senses." Next is *ilm-ul yaghin*, or "intellectual certainty." Finally, there is *hagh-ul yaghin*, or "revealed certainty." Certainty within the context of the seeker's

relationship with the sheikh falls into three stages. In the first stage, all the pupil can be sure of is that they yearn to be in the presence of the sheikh. Next, the seeker is certain that they understand the sheikh's instructions and intentions. And finally, the seeker is certain they are in sync with the sheikh's soul. This final stage is where the pupil can truly love and submit to the sheikh.

The Seventh Treatise: On Love

Chapter One. Introduction to Love

1 *Ashagha* is an Arabic word for "love." It is a kind of ivy plant that wraps itself around strong and healthy trees, feeds of them, and eventually kills them, for they become hollowed from within. The Sufis argue that divine love works in the same way. The Sufi guide's task is to create spiritual curiosity and then protect and nourish it until it grows into interest, infatuation, obsession, and finally, love. Through love, submission is obtained, and the lower self with its worldly desires is annihilated.

Chapter Two. On the Levels of the Shadows of Love

1 In Persian, this state is called *bast*. It is when one experiences the presence of God and feels union with Him.

2 In Persian, this state is called *ghabz*. It is when one feels separated and abandoned by God.

The Eighth Treatise

Chapter One. On the Ethical Codes of the Sufis

1 *Wuzu*, or "ablution," is, in the Islamic tradition, performed every time one stands to pray. It involves washing the hands, the face, the forearms, the crown of the head, and finally, the feet. The symbolism of washing these body parts, according to the Sufis, is that one must cleanse oneself of all worldly things when standing before God.

2 *Salat*, or "prayer," comes from the root word *sal*, "to join." The goal of prayer for the Sufis is to attain oneness with God.

Chapter Two. On the Benefit of Traveling

1 Due to the Sufi path's immense physical, emotional, intellectual, and spiritual difficulties and hardship, Sufi masters have always encouraged seekers to form friendships in spirit. The masters have repeatedly stressed that no one can journey and survive the Path without a guide and friendships.

Chapter Three. On the Codes of Conduct in the Khaneghah

1 *Khaneghah* is a Persian word that means a place where food and tea is served. It is unclear as to the origination of *khaneghah*. Some have suggested that the first was built at the request of Prophet Mohammad. Others have said that because the Sufis refused all things worldly and took a vow of poverty, they had no place to gather. Those with wealthy and were impressed by the Sufis' religious passion and sincerity built gathering places for them, and called it *khaneghah*. The great twelfth-century Sufi Attar, in his work, *Tazkerat ul-oliya* (Memorial of the saints), has suggested the first *khaneghah* was built by a Christian prince who was profoundly impressed with the warm and soulful interaction of the two Sufis.

Chapter Four. On Causing Another Dervish Sorrow

1 *Gham*, *Hozn*, or "sorrow," is one of the most critical stages of the Sufi path. This sorrow is the seekers' understanding that the physical world is not their *home* and their yearning to be united with God. This sense of homelessness births inner poverty, humility, silence, and submission. The great Sufi poet Hafez believed that when God loves a seeker, He commands His angels to sew spiritual sorrow in their hearts, which will then open the gates to prayer and union with Him.

Chapter Five. On Ecstatic Dancing

1 According to the Sufi tradition, *sama'a*, or "ecstatic dancing," popularized as the Whirling Dervishes, originated with the great Sufi poet and teacher Rumi. One day, as he was walking through town, he heard the blacksmiths hammering in such a melodic way that

he suddenly fell into an ecstatic state, or *bast*. According to some accounts, he whirled or danced for nearly three hours.

Chapter Six. On Eating

1 Nasafi refers to Attar's *Tazkerat ul-oliya* (Memorial of the saints) and Hajwiri's *Kashf al-mahjoob* (Revelation of the veiled).

Chapter Seven. On Asceticism and Discipline

1 According to the great eleventh-century Persian Sufi teacher Abdullah Ansari, the seeker's relationship with their master is one of the most mysterious aspects of Sufism. The seeker is gradually moved toward loving the teacher because they embody divine qualities. However, according to Ansari, the seeker at the same time moves toward having some negative emotions toward the guide, such as resentment, jealousy, anger, and hate. This is because of the growing conflict between the desires of the body and the desires of the soul. Hence the pupil stands amid certainty and doubt, joy and despair, and love and hate. According to Ansari, due to the immense love that the pupil has toward the sheikh, they will continue to serve him.

Chapter Eight. On Speech

1 The relationship between the seeker and the teacher's instructions or wisdom, whether through speech or otherwise, falls into three stages. The seeker has and can have no real understanding of the Path or the teacher's instructions or intentions. The pupil has a collection of raw and unrefined assumptions and superstitions about themselves, the sheikh, the Path, and God. In the next stage, the teacher is no longer interested in inspiring their pupil through emotions. Instead, they demand that their pupil understand the lectures and the instructions therein. That is inspiration through the intellect. In the final stage, the pupil has reached a level of emotional, intellectual, and spiritual maturity wherein they experience the teacher's instruction and sermon through their *nafs al-mutmainnah*, or "soul." This is the stage when the pupil and the sheikh unite through spirit.

The Ninth Treatise: On Maturity and Freedom

Chapter One. On the Meaning of Maturity and Freedom

1 For the Sufis, it is only through *nafs al-mutmainnah*, or "submission to the will of God or the sheikh," that maturity and freedom are attained. Any seeker having reached this stage has the power to filter and categorize the sensory experiences properly. Also, at this stage, the seeker can transform all things secular and profane into sacred and profound. In this way, God's presence can be seen and felt everywhere and in everything.

Chapter Two. On the Freedom and Maturity of Human Beings

1 According to the Sufis, one must want and, if possible, have the best of everything that the physical world offers. However, attachment to what one has must never be formed. In attachment, they argue, idols of worship are created that cause one to stray from the Path.

2 *Malamatiya*, meaning "Blameworthy," was a Sufi branch that came into existence in Iran around the ninth or tenth century. They refused to carry any money, for they believed money births desires that would turn into wants and then needs, which is a form of enslavement. They were also extremely against social status and wealth, as they believed one's status and identity should solely rest in God's hands.

The Tenth Treatise: On the Lesser World as a Representation of the Greater World

Chapter One. On the Greater and the Lesser Worlds

1 God informs the angels that he will create man (Quran 7.11; 15.28; 38.71) and that he will breathe his spirit into man (Quran 15.29; 38.72). The angels ask why he would make someone who would cause mischief and shed blood while the angels sing God's praises; God answers, "I know what ye know not" (Quran 2.30); then he asks the angels to tell him the names, but they are unable (Quran 2.3 1–32). Then he asks Adam to tell them the names (Quran 2.33). Adam does so, and God says to the angels, "Did I not tell you that I know the

secrets of heavens and earth and I know what ye reveal and what ye conceal?" (Quran 2.33). God tells the angels to bow down before Adam (Quran 2.34; 7.11; 18.50), prostrate themselves to Adam (Quran 20.116), or to fall in obeisance before him (Quran 15.29; 38.72).

Chapter Two. On the Action of God and the Action of God's Deputy

1 Nasafi and other Sufi greats, such as Rumi and Ibn al-Arabi, can be considered pantheists, believing that all things possess a divine spark within. This does not conflict with the concept of monotheism. *Zikr*, or the chanting of "La ilaha illa-llah," is, in Ibn al-Arabi's interpretation, just that: there is nothing but God.

Chapter Four. On Adam and Eve

1 In the Islamic tradition, God or Allah has one hundred names or attributes. Ninety-nine of those names or attributes are known, such as Merciful and Compassionate. One name, however, remains hidden, which God reveals only to the seeker. The Sufis believe that all the ninety-nine names exist in human beings. Only the saints, sages, and prophets, through rigorous training, understand and express these attributes appropriately and consistently. Hence the more attributes one possesses and manifests, the more divine one becomes.

Chapter Five. On the Manifestation of Hell and Paradise

1 In the Sufi tradition, the presence of the sheikh, or the Sufi master, is a symbol of paradise, for in him, the seeker can find such qualities as wisdom, solace, silence, mercy, compassion, and forgiveness.

The Eleventh Treatise: On Earthly, Heavenly, and Celestial (Intelligent) Realms

Chapter One. On the World

1 The great Greek philosopher Plato had argued that the physical world has its roots in the world of ideas, in which all things exist in utter perfection. The kind of beauty or perfection that human beings yearn for

can never be obtained in the physical world because it can only offer imperfect images or shadows of beauty or perfection. Because of this, the human being cannot but be in a perpetual state of dissatisfaction.

Chapter Two. A Further Discussion of the Physical, Heavenly, and Intelligible Realms

1 For Muslims, Mohammad is the representation of the perfected human being. According to the Sufis, he was a celestial man, a heavenly man, a physical man, and an earthly man and therefore was able to function in all four worlds harmoniously. He had divine experience and wisdom and knew how to apply the wisdom to the social and political realm.

Chapter Five. On Advice

1 "But seek first the kingdom of God and his righteousness, and all these things will be added to you" (Matthew 6:33 ESV). This saying, which is attributed to Jesus, is comparable to Nasafi's words here. Being in the presence of a sheikh who embodies divine qualities and being disciplined by him moves the seeker toward self-knowledge and God-knowledge and lessens the desire for material and worldly things.

The Twelfth Treatise: On Heavenly, Angelic, and Physical Realms: Part One

Chapter One. On the Nature of the Heavenly Realm

1 The great Sufi poet Rumi, in his *Masnavi*, likens the Sufi to an alchemist because he sees, feels, and understands that God has created the physical world and therefore has the essence of divinity. In this way, all physical experiences become a source of transformation.

Chapter Two. On Being, Nonbeing, and Love

1 *Ishgh*, or "love," occupies a significant place in Sufism. Rumi considers it mysterious and magical and sees it as descending upon human beings from the heavens. It can be experienced but can never be spoken of, as it is far too sacred to be embodied by language or human thought.

In one of his most beautiful poems regarding Ya'aghoub (Jacob) and Yousof (Joseph), Hafez comments that all human beings are like Ya'aghoub, having recognized and experienced the beauty of Yousof in some shape or form. This recognition and experience produce a kind of love that the human being desires to constantly experience.

2 According to Rumi, there are two sets of the five senses, and each set has a different function. The physical senses are seeing, smelling, hearing, tasting, and touching; they create intimacy and attachment and even inspire aspects of love between the human being and the contents of the physical world. The second set of senses belongs to the heart and only the spiritually evolved and mature can possess them to use the materials of physical world to find and create intimacy and union with God.

Chapter Three. On Advice

1 The concept of impermanence related to all things physical is a common theme in such major religious traditions as Hinduism, Buddhism, Taoism, Confucianism, Judaism, Christianity, and Islam. They all argue that attachment to anything physical will ultimately lead to disappointment, pain, and suffering. Human beings, by nature, desire stability and permanence. However, since the physical world is always in a state of change, stability is never found, and if by chance it is found, it is short-lived. Human relationships and attachments to the physical world give birth to an array of passionate emotions such as desire, hope, frustration, confusion, anxiety, love, envy, jealousy, and anger, which birth inner conflict and chaos. The spiritual sages have always counseled human beings to be mindful of the physical world's nature and its impact on the human psyche and spirit.

The Thirteenth Treatise: On the Celestial, Angelic, and Physical Realms: Part Two

Chapter One. On Unity

1 According to the grand sheikh of the Sufi tradition Ibn al Arabi, due to human beings' physical makeup, one cannot but experience unity

and municipality, wholeness and fragmentation. This is because human being cannot but constantly experience emotional, intellectual, and spiritual *ghabz* and *bast*—contraction and expansion or the feelings of connectedness and disconnectedness.

Chapter Two. On the Night of Revelation

1 *Laylat-al-ghadr*, "the Night of Power," is one of the holiest nights in the Islamic tradition. It was during this night that Prophet Muhammad was visited by the angel Gabriel (Jibrail), who revealed the initial contents of the Quran to him. The Sufis argue that seekers can only break their fasting when they too have had a *Laylat-al-ghadr* experience. In other words, the seekers' journey toward self-discovery and God-discovery can only reach a resting place when they have found what they have been searching for.

The Twenty-Second Treatise: On Heaven and Hell

Chapter One. On Heaven and Hell and Adam and Eve

1 There are several different interpretations of Adam and Eve in the Sufi tradition. One interpretation is that Adam represents physical desires, whereas Eve represents the spiritual. Adam generally overshadows Eve simply because the five senses and what they consider pleasurable are more accessible. Consequently, Eve cannot but remain hidden. It is only through the guidance of the serpent, the Sufi teacher, that Eve can surface. Another interpretation is that Adam was the first perfect man. Because of Eve, Adam was expelled from paradise due to choosing a short-term, temporary pleasure (the eating of the apple) over the eternal joys of paradise. Realizing the barrenness of physical life or temporary desires and pleasures, he pleaded with God to teach him how to return to paradise. Following the instruction of God, he was finally admitted.

Chapter Two. On the Gates of Heaven and Hell

1 All desires fall into five stages: the initiation, the rite of passage, the completion, the dissatisfaction, and finally, the indifference. The first

stage of desires is the infancy stage. This is an initiation, where one or more of the senses, through interaction with the physical world, becomes inspired and attracted to what was experienced. This inspired experience births a desire. Should the experience not be a passing desire but one that the individual wishes more of, then a journey toward fulfilling the desire begins. The second stage is when the desire has turned into want and need. These latter components—want and need—transform the human being into a political animal simply because they are forced to find ways to obtain the desire. Since every desire comes with a price tag, the individual is ultimately forced into becoming aware of whether they have the necessary physical, emotional, mental, and spiritual resources or funds to pursue the object of desire. The third stage is reaching the "promised land." That is, after perhaps a long and arduous journey, one has finally reached the object of desire. This is a stage where the individual rests in the object of one's desire. At this point, the individual's journey toward the desire has ended, and the journey toward enjoying the object of one's desire begins. This enjoyment has physical, emotional, mental, and even spiritual rewards that the individual basks in. The fourth stage is when the individual is overexposed to the object and feels saturated by the experience. That is, once the object of desire has been reached and a fair amount of pleasure has been extracted from it, one begins to feel that the object fails to create the excitement that it once did. This brings about a state of dissatisfaction. The fifth and final stage is when indifference sets in where the individual has lost all interest in the object that he or she once desired and its presence or absence matters very little.

Chapter Three. On the Stages of Heaven and Hell

1 In the Sufi tradition, it is believed that when God asked His creation who was willing to hold and carry His presence within, only the human being volunteered without being aware of what they had agreed to. This agreement became the source of both blessings as well as curses, joy as well as sorrow. Having the Kingdom of God within

them blessed the human being with moments filled with the divine presence, which created for the human being a sense of harmony, unity, and wholeness. These moments, however, were never meant to last, since divine love and beauty cannot be captured or possessed by human beings. The loss of experiencing God's presence created a feeling of separation and abandonment, which plunged the human being into frustration, grief, loneliness, anger, and despair. This, according to the Sufis, is the burden that human beings are born with and must carry throughout their lives.

Further Readings

Books in Persian

Ansari, Abdullah. *Kashf ul-asrar* [Quran's secrets unveiled]. Tehran: Amir Kabir, 1980.

Attar, Fariduddin. *Tazkerat ul-oliya* [Lives of Muslim saints and mystics]. Tehran: Zavar, 1982.

Bokhara'e, Ahmad Ali. *Farhang Ash'ar* [Hafez dictionary of Hafez's poems]. Tehran: Elmi, 1986.

Heravi, Hossein Ali. *Sharhe Ghazaliyate Hafez* [Commentary of Hafez's poems]. Tehran: Nashr No, 1982.

Nasafi, Aziz ul-Din. *Inson al-kamel* [*The Perfect Being*]. Tehran: Tahouir, 1984.

———. *Maghsad al-ghasee* [The sublime destination]. Tehran: Zavar, 1980.

Recommended Books

De Hartmann, Thomas, and Olga De Hartmann. *Our Life with Mr. Gurdjieff.* Sandpoint, ID: Sandpoint Press, 2008.

Field, Reshad. *The Invisible Way*. London: Harper & Row, 1979.

———. *The Last Barrier*. London: Harper & Row, 1977.

Izutsu, Toshihiko. *Sufism and Taoism*. Berkeley: University of California Press, 1983.

Lefort, Rafael. *The Teachers of Gurdjieff.* London: Victor Gollancz, 1971.

Ouspensky, P. D. *In Search of the Miraculous*. Eugene, OR: Harvest Books, 2001.

Shah, Idries. *The Commanding Self.* London: Octagon Press, 1994.

———. *Learning How to Learn*. London: Octagon Press, 1987.

———. *The Sufis*. London: Octagon Press, 1989.

Tweedie, Irina. *Daughter of Fire*. Grass Valley, CA: Blue Dolphin, 1987.